Rivers in World History

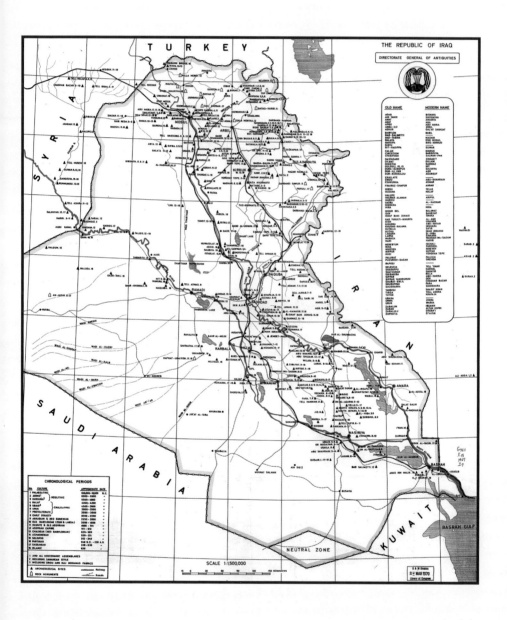

THE REPUBLIC OF IRAQ

DIRECTORATE GENERAL OF ANTIQUITIES

SCALE 1:1,500,000

THE
TIGRIS & EUPHRATES
RIVER

Shane Mountjoy

Series Consulting Editor
Tim McNeese

CHELSEA HOUSE
PUBLISHERS
A Haights Cross Communications Company
Philadelphia

FRONTIS: The sources of the Tigris and Euphrates Rivers lie within 50 miles of one another in eastern Turkey. The rivers flow southward on a parallel track through northern Syria and Iraq before emptying into the Persian Gulf.

CHELSEA HOUSE PUBLISHERS

VP, NEW PRODUCT DEVELOPMENT   Sally Cheney
DIRECTOR OF PRODUCTION   Kim Shinners
CREATIVE MANAGER   Takeshi Takahashi
MANUFACTURING MANAGER   Diann Grasse

Staff for THE TIGRIS AND EUPHRATES RIVERS

EXECUTIVE EDITOR   Lee Marcott
EDITOR   Christian Green
PRODUCTION EDITOR   Noelle Nardone
PHOTO EDITOR   Sarah Bloom
SERIES AND COVER DESIGNER   Keith Trego
LAYOUT   21st Century Publishing and Communications, Inc.

A Haights Cross Communications ⌁ Company ®

First Printing

9 8 7 6 5 4 3 2 1

Library of Congress Cataloging-in-Publication Data

Mountjoy, Shane, 1967–
   The Tigris and Euphrates rivers/Shane Mountjoy.
      p. cm.—(Rivers in world history)
   Includes bibliographical references and index.
   ISBN 0-7910-8246-6
   1. Tigris River—Juvenile literature. 2. Euphrates River—Juvenile literature.
I. Title. II. Series.
DS49.7.M695 2005
956.7—dc22

                                                          2004019396

All links and Web addresses were checked and verified to be correct at the time of publication. Because of the dynamic nature of the Web, some addresses and links may have changed since publication and may no longer be valid.

CONTENTS

1

The Twin Rivers of the Eastern Fertile Crescent

One rarely hears the Tigris and Euphrates Rivers mentioned individually. The two rivers almost seem as one. Biblical references usually list them together; each holds a place in the story of the Garden of Eden. When the rivers are mentioned in a historical context, it is almost unheard of to find either river discussed without the other. The land between the two waterways is almost mythical. It is believed by most to be the birthplace of civilization and by some to be the birthplace of humanity. The rivers themselves, as they flow toward the Persian Gulf, join together and flow as one for some 120 miles. The land lying between the two waterways is a vital part of the eastern Fertile Crescent, the region known as Mesopotamia. *Mesopotamia*, which is derived from Greek, means the "land between the rivers"—the Tigris and Euphrates Rivers.[1] In many respects, the history, the waters, and the tale of these two rivers are intertwined and inseparable. Theirs is a shared story.

Today, the Tigris and Euphrates begin less than 50 miles from one another. The two rivers travel south and eastward and then join together below Al Qurna before reaching the Persian Gulf, forming what is commonly called the *Shatt al-Arab* or the Arabic River. Here, the two rivers, historically inseparable, become physically joined before they empty into the Persian Gulf. In their upper courses, the rivers diverge by as much as 250 miles near the border of Turkey and Syria before meeting in a shared flow toward the sea. Although the Upper Tigris is higher in elevation than the Euphrates, the situation is reversed when the two rivers reach southern Iraq. As a result, the canals that join the two rivers flow west to east and empty into the Tigris, not the Euphrates. The middle courses of the two rivers steadily move toward one another; each serving as a border to a triangular stretch of limestone desert called Al-Jazirah, which in Arabic means "the island." This area is the heart of Mesopotamia. The Tigris receives

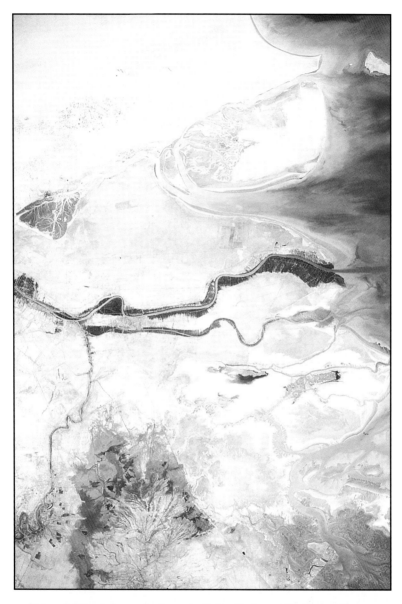

This satellite photograph shows both the Tigris and Euphrates Rivers flowing into the Persian Gulf. The two rivers come together below Al Qurna and form the Shatt al-Arab (Arabic River)—an area that has historically been a point of contention between Iran and Iraq for its easy access to the Persian Gulf.

water from the surrounding countryside, which has adequate precipitation; the Euphrates flows through bona fide desert lands. Interestingly, while flanking Al-Jazirah, the rivers' currents have cut deep beds into the rock. These beds, for the most part, have not deviated for centuries, and the middle courses of the Tigris and Euphrates Rivers of today look very much like they did before the age of the Sumerians. Near Fallujah and Baghdad, the rivers come within 30 miles of each other. Before the modern age of damming, it was not uncommon for the Euphrates, at flood stage, to flow overland to Baghdad and briefly meet up with the Tigris.

THE TIGRIS

The Tigris River, originating in eastern Turkey in the Taurus Mountains, flows some 1,180 miles in a southeasterly direction before joining the Euphrates near Al Qurna in southern Iraq. The Tigris flows through Turkey for 280 miles and for a 20-mile stretch helps form the border between Iraq and Syria; but the river is largely encompassed within the borders of Iraq. The Turkish portion of the river flows through constricted gorges that are clearly identifiable as a river valley. Rapids and ravines can be found along the river in its upper courses. Near the border of Syria and Iraq, the Al-Khabur River feeds the Tigris. One hundred miles downstream, a dam just north of Mosul restrains much of the river and helps prevent flooding. Then the Greater Zab and Lesser Zab add their waters to the Tigris, doubling its flow during the flood months (March and April). After the Tigris passes Tikrit, the landscape along its banks begins to level out to a wide, sloping plain that very slightly drops to sea level. As the river approaches the Persian Gulf, it becomes a winding waterway consisting of loops and arms that flow nowhere. There are even instances where the river isolates portions of land that used to carry the main flow.

As the Tigris passes through Iraq, it receives water from four tributaries: the Greater Zab, the Lesser Zab, the Adhem, and the Diyala. Consequently, the Tigris is prone to disastrous floods, unlike its partner river, the Euphrates. Each year, floodwaters raise the Tigris an average of $4^{1/2}$ to 9 feet. (In 1954, it rose 27 feet.) During flood season, the river flows swiftly, allowing local peoples to ship large loads weighing as much as 35 tons on wooden rafts called *kalaks*, which are positioned on floats made of goatskin and filled with air. During the flood season, these large rafts can travel the 275 miles between Mosul and Baghdad in just three or four days. After arriving in Baghdad, the kalaks are disassembled and the wood is sold. The goatskin floats are deflated and are transported by donkeys back upriver. The strong current does not permit much upriver traffic during the flood season. Throughout history, river trade was important for the region, but the Basra-Baghdad-Mosul Railway, constructed during the twentieth century, and the roads adjoining it, are now the conduit for most freight trade.

The flow of the upper portion of the Tigris is swift, preventing navigation north of Mosul. The mighty and ancient cities of Ashur, Calah, and Nineveh all flourished on the Tigris. Without the canal systems that extracted water from the river, the Sumerian civilization—which lasted from about 5000 B.C. to 1595 B.C.—might never have been. The ancient Sumerian city of Lagash (or Sirpurla), located near modern-day Shatra, received Tigris waters from a canal as early as 2400 B.C. The modern city of Baghdad, the capital of Iraq, lies on the western bank of the Tigris. Basra, the great port city of Iraq, is situated along the Shatt al-Arab. Saddam Hussein's hometown of Tikrit, which is a derivative of *Tigris*, is also on the river.

The land surrounding the river is alluvial—that is, the sediment deposited by the river enriches it through annual flooding in the same way that the Nile nourished Egypt prior to modern damming. Even with dams, some flooding still occurs today, but the floodwaters are controlled to prevent widespread damage. Throughout history, flooding has been both a blessing and a curse. The blessing is the fertile ground the flood creates—a yearly replenishing of nutrients or natural fertilizer. In the fifth century B.C., the Greek historian Herodotus described the effects of the flooding, which enabled a grain return of "two hundred fold and even up to three hundred fold." Herodotus added that "the blade of the wheat plant and the barley plant is often four fingers in breadth and the stalks of the millet and sesame are surprisingly tall." [2]

The curse is the natural disaster of excessive flooding, sure to come almost every year. All in all, however, the annual flooding has enabled the local peoples to domesticate, cultivate, and harvest grain products. Advancements in engineering technology—especially dams and barrages (earthen dams built to divert or hold back a river's flow)—have made it possible for the regular flooding to be harnessed for the good of the population.

Today, the Tigris River is frequently dammed throughout Turkey and Iraq. Damming provides some protection against the fierce floods that have plagued the Tigris for millennia. The construction of dams allows authorities to hold back rising floodwaters during the spring and also allows for the conservation of water for irrigation during the dry months of summer and fall.

Damming is not new to the region. In ancient times, the land between the Tigris and the Euphrates was an extensive series of canals used to irrigate the dry lands. Small boats also utilized the canal system, enabling limited transportation of goods and people. The canal system was created by the construction of dams. The ancient Greek geographer Strabo called them "artificial cataracts."[3] These dams were equipped with gates and sluices (valves) that could be opened or closed to adjust the amount of water flow. Dams were utilized for irrigation to supply necessary water for raising crops in the parched and arid lands flanking the Tigris River valley. Alexander the Great encountered such dams when he conquered the region in the fourth century B.C. In fact, the young Macedonian removed the dams of the Lower Tigris because they prevented his ships from moving down the river. (For additional information on this accomplished military commander, enter "Alexander the Great" into any search engine and browse the many sites listed.)

Since ancient times, two types of boats were used on the Tigris River and the Shatt al-Arab: riverboats and coracles. The riverboats are simply rectangular rafts that are used to float downstream. Riverboats may also be poled or towed upstream (by motorized boats). Coracles are round boats constructed from skins stretched over frames made of willow branches. Because they are somewhat more delicate than riverboats, coracles are mainly used for one-way, downriver traffic.

THE EUPHRATES

The Euphrates River, like its sister river to the east, flows from the highlands of eastern Turkey. It is the longest river of western Asia, flowing some 1,739 miles. The source of the river begins at the confluence of two rivers, the Murat (the eastern Euphrates) and the Karasu (the western Euphrates). The Murat emanates from Lake Van while the Karasu flows down from the mountains north of Ezerum, Turkey. The Euphrates is best described as a slow-moving, somewhat lethargic river that unhurriedly flows from mountainous regions across level plains on its way to the Persian Gulf. The Upper Euphrates runs through steep canyons and ravines before heading southwest across Syria, where the Khabur and Balikh Rivers—two rivers that also originate in Turkey—enter as tributaries. From this point until it unites with the Tigris below Basra, no other tributaries feed the Euphrates.

Since ancient times, the Euphrates has broken up into numerous channels at Basra. These channels formed wide-ranging marshlands. Until recently, the marshlands were fairly extensive, covering an area between 15,000 and 23,000 square miles—roughly the size of West Virginia.[4] Marsh Arabs inhabited this area until their opposition to Saddam Hussein's regime led to the systematic damming and draining of the marshlands.

Much of the Euphrates is non-navigable in its upper and lower courses. The upper courses are not conducive to boat traffic because of waterfalls and rapids; while the slowness of its current creates sandbars as it nears its mouth. The sand and silt-laden lower courses often require dredging to clear the waterways, limiting their use for transportation purposes. The middle course, situated on the level plains, is relatively shallow. Thus, navigation on the Euphrates River is possible only by very shallow draft boats, including kalaks, which are also used on the Tigris. Until the 1970s, people of the region also used *gufas*, which are the large circular coracles able to hold up to 20 passengers. These gufas are large baskets coated with bitumen, a naturally occurring, tar-like, petroleum-based material that is found in Mesopotamia (and throughout the world). Since ancient times, it has been used primarily for waterproofing.

Traffic on the Euphrates also includes *balams*, which are shallow, flat-bottomed boats. Other traditional watercraft used on the river are *muhaylahs* and *safinahs*, which are sailing craft measuring between 30 and 80 feet long. As outdated as these various boats may seem, they enable trade some 1,200 miles upstream to the city of Hit, Iraq, even though the city sits a

South of Basra, in southeastern Iraq, the Tigris and Euphrates break up into a series of channels and form extensive marshlands that once covered between 15,000 and 23,000 square miles. Iraqis known as the Madans, or Marsh Arabs, have lived in the area for thousands of years. Unfortunately, much of their land has been lost over the last decade, because Saddam Hussein diverted both the Tigris and Euphrates away from the area the Madans inhabit after they rebelled against the former Iraqi leader following the First Gulf War in 1991.

mere 176 feet above sea level. Upstream from Hit, the river is filled with rapids, preventing commercial navigation. The canal system linking the Euphrates with the Tigris also enables

LEGENDS OF A GREAT FLOOD FROM THE MIDDLE EAST

Virtually everyone in the Western world is familiar with the story of Noah and his ark, and the biblical account of a great, worldwide flood. The story of Noah, however, is neither the only account of a great flood nor the oldest. Many ancient civilizations have legends and myths about a flood so great that it covered the earth. These stories describe an overwhelming deluge that wiped out practically every living thing. They are found in texts and oral traditions of many ancient civilizations.

Despite the universality of accounts of legendary floods, the most famous story is that of Noah, which comes from the people of Mesopotamia. There is evidence that a great flood did indeed occur in the region. Archeological excavations in the Tigris-Euphrates River valley have revealed that between 4000 and 2000 B.C., the region was subjected to several floods. At least one of these was extremely powerful and destructive; it might have had such an impact that it became a theme in the literature of ancient writers.

Scholars believe that the Hebrew patriarch Abraham probably brought the Mesopotamian version of the flood story to Canaan (modern-day Palestine). They theorize that Hebrew writers later restructured the flood story as they wrote the Bible—recording creation, the birth of mankind, and other events. In the Genesis account, the entire world was flooded, and Noah and his family, along with two animals of every species, were saved only after building a great ark. Noah's flood lasted 40 days and the ark came to rest on the top of a mountain after the waters receded.

The Epic of Gilgamesh comes from the land of Sumer and is an early literary composition of the many adventures of an early Sumerian king. One of these adventures involves a flood story that has many similarities to and some notable differences from the biblical narrative. In this

the transportation of goods via river barges. Throughout history, even with innovations in boating and canals, the Euphrates has never served as a major conduit for commerce. Instead, the Tigris has been and continues to be the primary waterway in the region for commercial traffic.

account, dating back to nearly 2000 B.C., the hero is Utnapishtim. Utnapishtim—just as his Hebrew counterpart in the Genesis account—was advised by his god (in this case Ea) that a flood would destroy his city. To save himself and his family, Utnapishtim was told to construct a ship large enough for his family, his servants, and animals. Following a seven-day flood, the ship came to rest on a mountaintop. As in many other ancient Sumerian myths, Utnapishtim was seeking immortality, which the gods bestowed on him and his wife for their efforts.

The Chaldean form of the flood story closely resembles the Noah account. It centers on a man named Xisuthrus, who was warned by a god, Chronos, that a destructive flood would soon come. Following instructions from Chronos, Xisuthrus built a boat. He and his family, together with two of each animal species, took refuge in the boat. Following the flood, Xisuthrus released some birds, which returned twice with muddy feet. Released a third time, the birds did not return, and Xisuthrus surmised that the waters had receded. His family thankfully offered sacrifices to the gods for being rescued.

These legends of great floods are found in texts and oral traditions across the globe, including virtually every known civilization. Most accounts include stories of humankind becoming evil and a governing deity or deities who decide to punish humans or cleanse the earth. Some are saved in boats or are spared by climbing mountains; others find refuge in mountain caves. Like the Genesis account of Noah, some include mountains or birds that are released to test the floodwaters. Despite their differences, each story includes a great flood that kills virtually everyone, with the exception of two central figures (or a family) who later repopulate the earth.

THE CRADLE OF CIVILIZATION

The Euphrates and the Tigris (*Hiddekel* in Hebrew) Rivers are mentioned in the Genesis account of creation as two of four rivers flowing out of the Garden of Eden (Genesis 2:14). The creation account also describes the Tigris as the river in the east, which, of course, it is. Another biblical reference to the Euphrates (called *ha-nahar*, which simply means "the river" in Hebrew) denotes it as the eastern boundary of the land given to Abraham (the father of the Hebrew nation) and his descendants by God (Genesis 15:18).

It was along the Euphrates River that the first civilization blossomed some 60 centuries ago (about 4000 B.C.). Although the course of the river has changed over the millennia, many vital cities of the ancient world were developed on or very near the river. Among these were Eridu, Mari, Nippur, Shrrupak, Sippar, Urak, and the famed city of Ur. In the Euphrates River valley, the waters of the river were utilized for irrigation, allowing the great Babylonian and Assyrian Empires to emerge in the region. Later, as other empires developed, most notably the Egyptian and Roman, the Euphrates served as a border between the East and West.

The Tigris-Euphrates River valley is an elaborate collection of dams, canals, and irrigation channels. As previously noted, the canal system of the Tigris-Euphrates River system dates back hundreds of years and relies upon the dams and barrages that were built to control flooding and enable the construction of canals. In the third century A.D., the two rivers were connected by a series of five navigable canals. These canals—the Isa, Sarsar, Malik, Kutha, and Shatt al-Nil—allowed the region to be economically unified by enabling the transportation of goods and people. They are still in use today.

Mesopotamia—the land between the waters of the Tigris and Euphrates Rivers—is often called the birthplace of civilization. It has long been believed to be the home of the earth's first humans—the cradle of humanity. This term dates back to somewhere between the second and ninth century A.D., when the region was primarily inhabited by Arab Christians. It is believed that Muslims were still using this description when the Ottoman Empire was established in the early fourteenth century. When Protestant missionaries arrived in the area during the early 1800s, they often used the term as a means of identifying with and establishing relationships with the indigenous peoples.

The Tigris-Euphrates region has long been linked with ancient cultures. The world's first civilizations emerged in the region and some of the most impressive empires developed along the rivers' banks. Modern scholars believe that the first of these prominent Mesopotamian civilizations was that of Sumeria.

2

The Emergence of
the First Civilization

The Sumerian civilization of the Tigris-Euphrates River valley is the oldest of four early civilizations that developed around key rivers in their respective regions; the others being Shang China on the Yellow River; the Indus on the Indus River; and the Egyptian on the Nile River. Each of these ancient civilizations was situated within a fertile river valley. The Sumerians, like the Egyptians and those who lived along the Indus River, occupied an area surrounded by mountains, desert, and sea. The development and use of irrigation technology was vital for feeding the populations of these arid regions. Irrigation made intensive agriculture in these regions possible, but it also spurred diversification. As farmers tilled the soil, others were free to devote their energies to constructing buildings, temples, and cities. Eventually, this diversification became a catalyst for trade among the civilizations that were established along the various river valleys.

In Mesopotamia, the irrigation of the arid lands occurred naturally. Annual floods brought rich nutrients from the rivers' sediment to the surrounding plain. During the fourth millennium B.C., people began to discover ways in which to trap the water at flood stage for later use. Inhabitants also discovered *field agriculture*—the growing of crops from seeds, usually grains. Soon, these discoveries attracted other settlers to the region. As food became more readily available on the alluvial plains of the Tigris-Euphrates River valley, permanent communities were set up near the all-important rivers. Increasingly, early residents irrigated the land with river water, domesticated animals and crops, and generally accumulated more possessions. As food supplies increased, population also rose. This population growth was not necessarily a drain on the food economy. Instead, the excess food enabled a portion of the population to undertake other endeavors, none of which had anything to do with the cultivation or harvesting of food. The amassing of possessions signals the transition to a settled lifestyle. Pottery, tools, jewelry, buildings, and weapons are some of the most important and revealing artifacts from ancient civilizations.

Advances in mathematics grew out of the shift from a nomadic to a settled society and included the development of calendars (to determine seasons), measurements of distance (to divide property), and measurements of volume (to record amounts of seed or grain). As measurements became more exact and uniform, their use helped stimulate trade throughout the region.

Sumer was located in southern Mesopotamia on the southeastern tip of the Fertile Crescent, in what is modern-day Kuwait and northeastern Saudi Arabia. Much of what we know today of the Sumerians comes from archaeological finds, including thousands of clay tablets. For the most part, these artifacts have been unearthed in the past 200 years, with excavations and translation research first revealing the secrets of Sumerian culture in the nineteenth century.

The Sumerians called the land between the Tigris and Euphrates Rivers Sumer, or Shinar in Biblical references. Scholars do not know whether the Sumerians originated in Sumer or migrated to the area from some other region. We do know that, in contrast to the rest of the peoples in the region, they were not Semites—groups of nomads who migrated to the Fertile Crescent from the Arabian Peninsula and spoke one of the Semitic languages. (Although the term *Semitic* often refers to Jews, Arabs are also Semitic peoples). The Sumerians had a rather distinctive language, which is not related to any known tongue. If they were not native to Mesopotamia, then it is likely that they emigrated from Persia, probably no later than 4000 B.C. By about 3800 B.C., the Sumerians had wrested power from the Ubaidians and Semites who lived in Mesopotamia. It is believed that the Ubaidians had appeared in the region around 4500 B.C. and were named after the archaeological find at Al Ubaid, near the mouth of the Tigris-Euphrates River. Also a non-Semitic people, they had drained the marshes and introduced irrigated agriculture to the region, and had used their handcrafted products (including leather goods, metalwork, pottery, and woven items) to develop regional trade.

FARMING AND IRRIGATION

Farming techniques were acquired and diffused throughout the Middle East, especially in the Fertile Crescent, around 6500 B.C. These innovations allowed the nomads of the region to abandon their wandering lifestyle and settle in one location. Crops and animals were raised in one area, ending the nearly constant travel previously necessary to ensure a stable food supply.

By approximately 5000 B.C., the Tigris-Euphrates River valley was home to small groups of farmers who raised barley, peas, and wheat. Surprisingly, "even after thousands of years of domestication and farming, of the tens of thousands of edible plants species on earth, only about 600 were raised for food. Many were first grown in the Fertile Crescent."[5] Early farmers in the region had achieved irrigation by diverting small amounts of river waters to their fields. The Sumerians used this knowledge and refined it by constructing dams, digging canals, and draining marshes in order to cultivate their crops. Some scholars believe that the introduction of law and government came about in Sumerian culture because of large-scale irrigation projects that required a complex working relationship among many people. There is no doubt that the Sumerians established their own laws and that their institutions of government effectively served to coordinate and encourage irrigation farming.

The Sumerians proved capable of building better canals for irrigating their crops than those built by their predecessors. They upgraded roads by which they transported their crops to growing communities, usually by donkey or donkey-pulled wheeled carts. Once a dependable and consistent food source became available, the Sumerians began to turn their attention and energies to other pursuits. These other pursuits included architecture, writing, and construction. The Sumerians introduced the world's first arches, developed the world's first writing system, and built the world's first cities. Without the advancements they made in agriculture, it is unlikely the Sumerians would have established what many archaeologists believe to be the first civilization.

SUMERIAN CITIES

The Sumerians were unique because they were the first ancient civilization to build large, flourishing cities where thousands of people resided. Indeed, the word *civilization*, which is derived from an ancient word for "city," is used to describe a people who have developed communities with social and governmental institutions as well as advancements in arts and sciences. These early communities grew around temples and became the nuclei for city-states. Given the primitive state of communication and transportation, these city-states were probably the most likely kind of governable communities. The Sumerians had at least 12 such cities, the most famous of which was Ur, which is identified in Genesis as the city of Abraham. In time, Ur had a population of roughly 24,000 people.

By about 3500 B.C., Sumerian cities were more than just large simple farming communities. The people believed that a god or gods owned the land surrounding their cities. For this reason, there were no individually owned tracts of land. Instead, the land was cultivated by groups of people, overseen by priests who served the local gods. Crops, which included barley, beans, flax, grapes, olives, and wheat, were grown for the city inhabitants. Sumerians hunted and fished for food and also successfully domesticated donkeys, goats, and sheep. They

Sumer was made up of 12 city-states, including Kish, Lagash, Uruk, and Ur. The most important city-state was Ur, which at its height had a population of 24,000 and was an important center of Sumerian culture.

produced such an abundance of food that some members of their society were no longer needed to help produce it; instead devoting themselves to other callings, including the priesthood. Indeed, some historians believe that cities were constructed for the purpose of worship:

> One feeble voice raised in prayer might not reach the gods, but thousands would have a better chance of being heard. Early cities were completely surrounded by walls for

defense, and inside the walled city was another walled mini-city, the temple. Inside the temple walls was the most important building, the granary, where the city stored its food. This surplus of food made specialized labor possible because not everyone had to farm all the time. The community decided that their resources would be better spent if they had a priest or priestess to honor the gods full-time. This included preparing food offerings for them, honoring them with feasts on their special days, and sometimes inviting gods from other cities to visit. So, from the earliest civilizations, food, religion, and government were all connected. For whatever reason cities arose, they became centers of trade.[6]

Although built on an agricultural base, Sumerian society was composed of freemen, priests, slaves, soldiers, and commercial traders. At the center of each city was the local god's temple. Over time, the temples became more imposing and resembled mountains. Thus the *ziggurat*, or "holy mountain," with its stair-step appearance, became the central focus of these communities; other buildings were constructed around them. British archaeologist Sir Leonard Woolley was instrumental in excavating the Sumerian city of Ur and its impressive ziggurat. Woolley later wrote, "It seems incredible that such a wilderness should ever have been habitable for man, and yet the weathered hillocks at one's feet cover the temples and houses of a great city."[7]

Despite the harsh climate, ziggurats were built and people were drawn to the cities that grew up around them. In time, rulers emerged who controlled the all-important irrigation systems for the local population. It is also likely that the irrigation systems, which helped create additional surpluses in the food supply, fed the rulers and other non-food-producing members of society such as priests, artisans, and craftsmen.

Trade prospered as the Sumerians cultivated a wide-ranging commercial system that included importing goods via ships in the Persian Gulf.

The Sumerians not only crafted the world's first civilization, they also introduced some key inventions that helped transform the way humankind lived. These inventions included potter's wheels, metalworks, and wheeled carts. (Although Chinese carts may predate those found in Mesopotamia, the Sumerians apparently developed theirs independently). Other innovations include the first lunar calendar, which was later embraced by the Semites, Egyptians, and Greeks as their own cultures evolved. The Sumerians also produced and utilized standard measures, including units of area, capacity, and length. Sumerians did not coin money but instead relied upon standard weights of silver to serve as the means of exchange. The mina was their standard weight and was equal to 60 shekels (about a pound).

WRITING

Ancient civilization refers to the 3,600 years beginning in approximately 3100 B.C. and continuing to the fall of the Roman Empire in A.D. 476. It was during this time that human-kind began preserving a written record of achievements. In particular, ancient civilizations were foundational societies that built city-states, nation-states, and empires. The Sumerians exhibited each of the necessary characteristics of civilization and were the first to record their achievements in written form, albeit on tablets of clay.

Perhaps to keep an accurate account of their measurements and business transactions, the Sumerians employed clay tablets to record their writing. Archaeologists believe that the Ubaidians may have been the first to use some of the elements of writing, but the Sumerians soon refined their rather primitive writing methods, standardized them, and began to use them for record keeping and other purposes. Thus, even though scholars do not know who developed the first writing, the Sumerians were the first to develop a uniform system of writing.

Writing was achieved by making impressions on wet clay tablets that, when baked dry, preserved the script. The impressions were made with the end of a reed with three corners. The reed was used to draw straight lines and make impressions that left wedge-shaped marks, with each sign or set of marks representing one sound, object, or idea. These pictographs were the early form of what we now call *cuneiform*, which is Latin for "wedge-shaped." The clay tablets on which these pictographs were drawn were no doubt bulky and difficult to use; they are also difficult to reconstruct if broken. One advantage they have, however, is their amazing longevity, which enables modern scholars to read Sumerian writings that date back before 3000 B.C. The adoption of cuneiform by the Babylonians and Assyrians ensured its spread into Anatolia, Armenia, Iran, and Syria. (For additional information on this ancient form of communication, enter "cuneiform writing" into any search engine and browse the many sites listed.)

The cuneiform system of writing was extremely complex. There were literally thousands of groups of wedges and the process of combining them into symbolic representations of ideas or concepts was extremely labor intensive. Since cuneiform was so complicated, learning it proved to be somewhat difficult and problematic. Children studied at a temple school where they were given clay tablets with an instructor's writing on the left side. They attempted to reproduce the instructor's marks on the right side. Mistakes could be "erased" by smoothing out the clay and impressing the entry again. Many student copies of first chapters from virtually every notable Sumerian work have been discovered, but it seems that few managed to finish copying entire lengthy compositions, because only a small number of finished copies have been unearthed.

Sumerian writing, known as cuneiform, probably developed as a means to recognize private property. However, the Sumerians wrote about many different topics on clay tablets, including history, medicine, legal codes, and mathematics. A pen made from a sharpened reed was used to create horizontal rows of wedge-shaped marks in the wet clay and the tablets could be made permanent by firing them in a kiln.

The Sumerians had a deep-rooted belief in private property. If the surviving clay tablets offer any insight, then writing may have been developed simply to keep records of ownership. Documents listing personal possessions include practically everything, including shoes. Scribes who served as notaries worked near city gates and dutifully recorded details of all business transactions. Parties to a contract would use a seal, usually an engraved stone or metal cylinder that was rolled over the wet tablet, to create a written record of the deal. Over time, cuneiform, in the same ways we use modern writing, came to be used for virtually every conceivable function.

Sumerians certainly used cuneiform to advance mathematics. Some of the clay tablets diagram the stars and lay out a system of dividing a circle into 60 equal units (and later into 360 degrees), from which is derived our modern system of hours, minutes, and seconds. It seems that the Sumerians based their number system on 10, then multiplied 10 by 6, equaling 60. Thereupon the system alternated between multiples of 10 and 6 (600, 3600, etc.). The number 60 holds some distinct benefits in mathematical calculations because it is divisible by 2, 3, 4, 5, 6, 10, 12, 15, 20, and 30. In fact, it is from the Sumerians that we have the word *dozen*, which is one-fifth of 60.

Not all Sumerian writing dealt with numbers or record keeping. The Sumerians wrote about many different things on their clay tablets: history, medicine, legal codes, and more. Surviving tablets include poetry, much of which deals with the Sumerians' religious beliefs and their many gods.

RELIGION

The Sumerians were polytheistic, that is, they believed in many different gods. In fact, the Sumerians believed that spirits inhabited virtually everything, including nature and objects they themselves had created. It was a somewhat mystical view that helped them explain the world around them and the way the world worked. For the Sumerians, the sky, the earth, water, the stars, the sun, and the moon were all gods that possessed humanlike emotions and interacted with each other much like humans. Each of these gods was tied to and originated from a specific city, and was worshiped in the local ziggurat and in small shrines in homes. Reeds grew because a goddess of reeds caused them to grow; beer was distilled, but the production process worked only because of a goddess of beer. Successes and failures of annual harvests were explained by the Sumerians' belief in the gods. The soil produced crops because a male god mated with his goddess wife or the gods temporarily died during the hot, dry months of the year. Thus, when the ground again bore crops in the fall, these "dead" gods were considered resurrected. The return of foliage served as their new year, which was observed by singing and music in their ziggurat temples.

Other Sumerian beliefs reflected their experiences in Mesopotamia. For instance, because they knew they could dig just a few feet before finding water, beliefs, myths, and theories related to the nature of Earth were soon recorded. Sumerians believed that since water was so close to the surface, the earth was simply a large disk floating on the sea, or *Nammu*. From the eternal Nammu came fish, birds, and any animals they saw in the marshlands. Because they viewed Nammu as a god, in their view of creation, water was the source of all life. Considering their location in the arid land between the Tigris and Euphrates Rivers and their dependence upon those rivers for life, this creation view, which denotes the importance of water, mirrors their experience in Mesopotamia.

As part of their creation beliefs, the Sumerians believed that heaven was a male god (An), while the earth was a female goddess (Ki). The offspring from these two, Enlil, was the god of wind and storm, and was also responsible for making rain and creating day and night. They believed that Ki and Enlil provided the circumstances that made possible the creation of plants and animals. Specifically, the Sumerians believed that Enlil caused seeds to grow and that after giving form to humans, he gave them the "breath of life"—a striking parallel to the Genesis account of creation in which mankind was given the "breath of life" (Genesis 2:7).

Like the people of many ancient civilizations, the Sumerians also believed that humankind existed in order to serve the gods. This service was accomplished through offering sacrifices and prayers. Because they believed the gods held power over the past and the future, they attributed all acquired knowledge to their gods. Thus, they did not believe that their accomplishments were of their own doing but were rather gifts from the gods. Nor did they comprehend the ideas of social or technological progress. Because the gods provided everything, they saw no need to acquire new knowledge. They were essentially a society with remarkable achievements whose belief system required that they remain almost stationary.

Despite the limitations imposed upon them by their early religious beliefs, Sumerians did change over time. Their religious stories also changed; revised as new elements were added to old narratives. These changes were not attributed to priests or sages; they were explained away as new revelations from one or more of their many gods. The underlying theology remained relatively constant: Humankind relied upon the gods for all that they were and had. Within this climate, there was little room for questioning faith. The religious climate of the Sumerian cities, though advocating the belief in many gods and goddesses, was not one of religious freedom. If the stories indicated something must be done, then people adhered to the requirements imposed by the gods or goddesses. The gods and goddesses had supplied them with life, knowledge, and all their needs. In return, residents of the city-states were to proffer sacrifices and offer prayers to the gods and goddesses. By the middle of the second millennium B.C., however, individualism had influenced Sumerian belief to the point that it was acceptable for individuals to enter into covenants with gods. Each man adopted his own god, in addition to the city's god, to whom he prayed and offered sacrifices.

THE LEGACY OF SUMER

Sumerian society revolved around 12 city-states: Adab, Akshak, Bad-tibira, Kish, Lagash, Larak, Larsa, Nippur, Sippar, Umma, Uruk, and Ur. Scholars believe that eight kings ruled Sumer before the time of a great flood—which is referred to in ancient Mesopotamian writings. Following the famous deluge, various city-states took turns as the provisional capital until around 2800 B.C., when Etana, king of Kish, united all the city-states under his rule. Following his death, the city-states fought among themselves for domination, resulting in an overall decline of the region, leaving it ripe for invasion. Despite their many great achievements in technology and culture, disunity and rivalry among Sumerian city-states continued until about 2300 B.C., when a Semitic invader named Sargon entered the region and conquered them.

Sargon, an Akkadian, rose to power from an obscure and humble background. According to a legend recorded in the seventh century B.C., his mother gave up Sargon in a most unique way:

> My changeling mother conceived me, in secret she bore me. She set me in a basket of rushes, with bitumen she sealed my lid. She cast me into the river, which rose not over me. The river bore me up and carried me to Akki, the drawer of water . . .[8]

Despite Sargon's supposed humble beginnings, he enjoyed a distinct advantage over the Sumerians—he led standing and well-trained armies. The Sumerians had maintained only citizen armies, and these proved no match for the Akkadians. Mesopotamia became a part of their empire, which reached all the way to the Mediterranean Sea. Having conquered the Sumerians, Sargon built a new city, Akkad (near modern-day Baghdad), to serve as his capital, but Akkadian control continued for less than a century.

Ur, which was established around 2500 B.C., is mentioned throughout the Bible and is said to be the home of Abraham. The site was discovered in the nineteenth century, but an account of its history was not constructed until British archaeologist Sir Leonard Woolley excavated the city in the 1920s and 1930s.

After the decline of Akka, the Sumerians, under the leadership of Ur, again enjoyed supremacy in the region. Ur's preeminence lasted for about a century—approximately 2150 to 2050 B.C.—and Sumerian culture flourished under its leadership. Ultimately, the waters of the Euphrates River that had allowed the Sumerians to build cities and erect a civilization, proved to be their downfall. The Euphrates changed course and began flowing farther to the west, leaving the formerly thriving cities to stand desolate in the desert. River water for irrigation also led to salinization, which depleted the soil's fertility and decreased agricultural production. Other evidence suggests that a volcanic eruption in Turkey might have temporarily disrupted weather patterns at the outset of a natural but lengthy drought that lasted 300 years. The population was forced to leave in order to survive. Remnants of the once flourishing cities still stand today, monuments to the past of a great and thriving civilization that once lived on the alluvial plain of a great river.

The Sumerians were eventually overrun by other neighboring powers, but their Semitic successors adopted much of their civilization. As the independent Sumerian cities steadily lost their autonomy, their language outlived their culture. Under waves of successive invasions and conquests, the Sumerian language survived and even thrived as the official language of business. Other cultural features, such as Sumerian religious beliefs, commercial structure, business practices, cuneiform writing, and law were adopted and diffused by the Akkadians, Babylonians, Assyrians, and Chaldeans.

3

Southern Mesopotamia: The Early Babylonian Empire

Today, in the deserts of Iraq, near the Euphrates River, stand the ruins of what was the ancient world's first truly dominant city. At its height, the city was called Bab-llu or "gate of the gods." The Hebrews called the city Babel; later, the Greeks and Romans called it Babylon. The countryside over which the city once ruled was known as Babylonia. Babylon existed for more than a 1,000 years as a minor village before being elevated, in 1894 B.C., to the capital of the Babylonian kingdom. Historian Joan Oates explains its rise to prominence:

> In 1894 B.C., an Amorite dynasty was founded at Babylon which was to bring that city to a pre-eminence it maintained, psychologically if not politically, for nearly 2,000 years. Up to this time . . . Babylon had made no mark on its country's history. Yet little over 100 years later this city ruled all Mesopotamia, albeit briefly.[9]

HAMMURABI

In 3000 B.C., Babylon was merely one of many city-states in the region that was ruled by a nomadic group of Syrian and Arabic tribes called the Amorites. Enjoying more than one turn as the region's foremost city, its initial period of glory came under the leadership of Hammurabi, the sixth ruler of the city in the Amorite line. Hammurabi is best known for his codification of laws, but he was also the ruler who made the city the cultural and religious center of the region. Hammurabi built palaces and temples and fortified the defensive bulwarks of Babylon. More importantly, Hammurabi instructed the city's priests to sustain Sumerian culture by preserving Sumerian writing. Temple priests meticulously reproduced Sumerian clay tablets, and Sumerian culture formed the basis of Babylonian civilization.

Hammurabi assumed the throne around 1792 B.C. and reigned for about 42 years. To secure his position and defend Babylon, he entered into a series of alliances and negotiated numerous trade agreements with neighboring city-states. These treaties ensured peace and a flourishing trade for his city-state. It was under Hammurabi that Babylon began to enjoy its first dynasty, which lasted about 300 years. Under Hammurabi's leadership, Babylon extended its control westward into present-day Syria and southward into Sumer. Hammurabi limited most of his military exploits to southern Mesopotamia because Assyria, a fierce and militaristic society, controlled northern Mesopotamia. Although Hammurabi did manage to temporarily force his rule over portions of the Assyrian Empire, Babylonian successes in northern Mesopotamia were mostly limited to his lifetime.

HAMMURABI'S LAWS

Hammurabi's greatest contribution was his collection and recording of the Babylonian legal code. Although the set of laws was essentially rewritten from previous compilations, the more comprehensive Code of Hammurabi brings to light key aspects of ancient Babylonian society. For instance, the code divided the populace into three distinct classes: nobles, freedmen, and slaves. Nobles were those with hereditary estates and enjoyed full civil rights. Nobles also had responsibilities and privileges pertaining to the aristocracy. The king, his court, high officials, professionally trained men, and craftsmen all belonged to this class.

Freedmen included those who might own land, but they were not allowed to leave it to their children. Generally, they were landless individuals who were forced to accept monetary compensation for injuries and suffering wrongdoing. This class also lived in a separate part of the city. In short, freedmen had their freedom but almost little else.

A stone engraving detailing Babylonian King Hammurabi's appointment as protector and lawgiver of his people by the god Marduk. Hammurabi created a code that addressed such criminal and civil laws as capital crimes, slander, and contract obligations. One such law—"an eye for an eye and a tooth for a tooth"—became a part of the Hebrew Bible's Torah's lexicon.

Finally, the code identified slaves, specifically those who were sold in the open market. Although serving as a slave to pay off debts was legal, it was for a fixed amount of time (three years). Most slaves were acquired through war. Under the code, a slave could own property, including other slaves. A slave's food, clothing, and medical costs were the responsibility of his master, but the latter also received any compensation paid for injury to the slave. Typically, the master would provide a wife (a slave-girl) for his male slave and even provide him with a house for which the slave paid rent. Any offspring belonged to the master. According to one account:

> Otherwise he might marry a freewoman (the children were then free), who might bring him a dower which his master could not touch, and at his death one-half of his property passed to his master as his heir. He could acquire his freedom by purchase from his master, or might be freed and dedicated to a temple, or even adopted, when he became a noble.[10]

In such cases, the slave no longer offered financial rewards for the master. Other provisions concerning slavery specified that if a slave ran away and was caught, "the captor was bound to restore him to his master, and the code fixes a reward of two shekels, which the owner must pay the captor."[11] Two shekels amounted to approximately 10 percent of the value of an average slave. Keeping an escaped slave for oneself or helping a slave escape was punishable by death. Slaves "bore an identification mark, which could only be removed by a surgical operation and which later consisted of his owner's name tattooed or branded on the arm."[12] Thus, for slaves, the code was a mixture of opportunities and restrictions.

Hammurabi seemed proud of the laws he had compiled and had them engraved in stone. In the epilogue to the code, he declared that he, "the protecting king" and "king of righteousness," had delivered "righteous" and "pious" laws in the code—laws that came from the gods themselves.[13] He further declared himself the "salvation-bearing shepherd, whose staff is straight," and who led by great wisdom over his people.[14] Hammurabi's rationale for creating the code, according to the epilogue, was so "that the strong might not injure the weak, in order to protect the widows and orphans."[15] It is not likely that he accomplished all that he intended through his code, but Hammurabi did gain lasting fame and recognition. His engraved statutes are today known around the world.

BABYLONIAN CULTURE AND SOCIETY

Under Hammurabi's rule, the Babylonian god Marduk was elevated to role of supreme deity. Sumerian myths were rewritten to recognize Marduk instead of Enlil as the god of creation, and the Babylonian primary female goddess, the ancient mother deity, was renamed Ishtar. Babylonians believed that Ishtar, who was the goddess of fertility, was capable of granting faithful worshippers children, crops, or lambs. Related to her fertility role, Babylonian myths named the hottest month of the summer after her son, Tammuz. Out of respect for Ishtar, people fasted until Tammuz reappeared (rose from the dead) and watered the parched soil of the region to restore green life to the dry and brown flora. The worship of Ishtar and Tammuz appears in Egyptian beliefs as Isis and Osiris, and subsequently in Greek mythology as Demeter and Persephone.

As long as Hammurabi ruled, Babylonia flourished economically. Situated in the midst of well-established trade routes, Hammurabi's Babylon rose to become a significant trading center, with Babylonian trade reaching westward to the Mediterranean Sea and southward to the Persian Gulf. Surplus crops enabled the Babylonians to trade for items not indigenous to the region. Because the crops that were grown on the irrigated plain of the Tigris-Euphrates River valley were the primary Babylonian exports, Hammurabi saw to it that the irrigation system was well cared for and maintained. Mesopotamian grain and cloth woven locally were used to

(continued on page 38)

THE CODE OF HAMMURABI

The most famous piece of surviving cuneiform writings is the set of laws known as the Code of Hammurabi. Hammurabi claimed that he was "the exalted prince, who feared God" who decided "to bring about the rule of righteousness in the land, to destroy the wicked and the evil-doers; so that the strong should not harm the weak; so that I should rule over the black-headed people like Shamash, and enlighten the land, to further the well-being of mankind."* Hammurabi believed that his chief god, Marduk, had appointed him as protector and lawgiver for his people, and he intended to rule justly. "When Marduk sent me to rule over men, to give the protection of right to the land, I did right and righteousness in . . . and brought about the well-being of the oppressed."**

The Code contains 282 provisions that cover a wide range of topics related to criminal and civil law: capital crimes, slander, contract obligations, wage rates, slaves, punishments, and others. Some of the laws are included in other ancient legal codes and are familiar to modern cultures. Among them, for example, we find "an eye for an eye and a tooth for a tooth." Numbers 196 and 200, included among the excerpts below may also be familiar to people of our time.***

6. If anyone steal the property of a temple or of the court, he shall be put to death, and also the one who receives the stolen thing from him shall be put to death.

22. If anyone is committing a robbery and is caught, then he shall be put to death.

55. If anyone open his ditches to water his crop, but is careless, and the water flood the field of his neighbor, then he shall pay his neighbor corn for his loss.

102. If a merchant entrust money to an agent (broker) for some investment, and the broker suffer a loss in the place to which he goes, he shall make good the capital to the merchant.

196. If a man put out the eye of another man, his eye shall be put out.

200. If a man knock out the teeth of his equal, his teeth shall be knocked out.

202. If any one strike the body of a man higher in rank than he, he shall receive sixty blows with an ox-whip in public.

203. If a freeborn man strike the body of another freeborn man of equal rank, he shall pay one gold mina.

205. If the slave of a freed man strike the body of a freed man, his ear shall be cut off.

215. If a physician make a large incision with an operating knife and cure it, or if he open a tumor (over the eye) with an operating knife, and saves the eye, he shall receive ten shekels in money.

218. If a physician make a large incision with the operating knife, and kill him, or open a tumor with the operating knife, and cut out the eye, his hands shall be cut off.

219. If a physician make a large incision in the slave of a freed man, and kill him, he shall replace the slave with another slave.

By modern standards, the code appears quite harsh, but the fact that Hammurabi sought to standardize punishments or that some injuries/infractions could be remedied by paying a fine was significant. The code recognized rights, at least at some level, for each class of the population (including slaves). At the close of the inscribed code, Hammurabi expressed his desire that his laws would last beyond his lifetime:

> In future time, through all coming generations, let the king, who may be in the land, observe the words of righteousness which I have written on my monument; let him not alter the law of the land which I have given, the edicts which I have enacted; my monument let him not mar. If such a ruler have wisdom, and be able to keep his land in order, he shall observe the words which I have written in this inscription; the rule, statute, and law of the land which I have given; the decisions which I have made will this inscription show him; let him rule his subjects accordingly, speak justice to them, give right decisions, root out the miscreants and criminals from this land, and grant prosperity to his subjects.[+]

Although his kingdom eventually fell and his descendants no longer ruled the land he had conquered, Hammurabi is still remembered today because of his great code. Thus, even though his kingdom died out, his reputation as a great lawgiver continues to survive.

* *http://www.fordham.edu/halsall/ancient/hamcode.html.*

** Ibid.

*** Examples of the Code of Hammurabi are excerpted from the Internet Source Book, which includes the code in its entirety. It was translated by L.W. King and may be found online at *http://www.fordham.edu/halsall/ancient/hamcode.html.*

+ Ibid.

(continued from page 35)

trade for livestock, precious metals, and gems. Archaeologists have unearthed tools, weapons, and building materials made from imported tin, iron, and copper. Decorative jewelry, including earrings, bracelets, and necklaces were made from imported jewels. Trees, which also had to be imported, provided the wood for ships and furniture.

The arts and sciences also flourished during Hammurabi's reign. Advancements in mathematics included tables used for calculating the square and cube roots of numbers. Astronomers made key discoveries in their field. Architecture reflected Babylon's rise to prominence; temples and palaces were built as tributes to the gods and the ruler. These temples became elaborate groupings of several buildings rather than just a single structure. Palaces reflected the newfound wealth of Babylonian ascendancy, each resembling a small city rather than a simple dwelling. The royal palace at Mari, for example, included bathrooms and a sewage system, and covered some seven acres. The homes of affluent people contained large wall murals. In addition, sculptures and scenes of everyday life were fashioned from clay and carved into stone. Some of these sculptures and carvings survive today. Literary tradition also prospered as poetry, religious beliefs, and Babylonian classics were written, revised, or copied. Indeed, Hammurabi's reign was generally a period of prosperity and advancement.

KASSITE RULE

Despite Hammurabi's prediction that Babylonia would last forever, his kingdom began losing territory almost immediately after his death in 1750 B.C. Hammurabi's line continued to rule for more than a century after his death, but Babylonia was reduced to the city of Babylon and a small amount of adjoining territory. Around 1600 B.C., Babylonia was attacked and plundered by the Hittites from Anatolia (Asia Minor). A few years later, the Kassites, who came from east of the Tigris and traced their ruling lineage to the mid-eighteenth century B.C., also ransacked Babylonia. Unlike the Hittites, however, the Kassites intended to stay. They established a line of rulers that lasted more than 400 years, until 1157 B.C. Thus, the first Babylonian dynasty ended within two centuries of Hammurabi's death.

Life for residents of Babylon under Kassite rule was little different than it had been prior to the Kassite invasion. The Kassites embraced most of Babylonian culture and maintained the traditional rights of citizens. Consequently, the Kassites never faced revolts, which allowed the ruling dynasty to enjoy an extensive reign in Babylon. The Kassites even managed to reclaim lost territory to the south, all the while unifying all of Babylonia. One of the key elements to Kassite success lay in foreign trade. Babylonia continued to enjoy the benefits of its location within the Middle East, acting as a kind of agent for overland trade between places as distant as Egypt to the west and India to the east.

The Kassites also emphasized the supremacy of one Babylonian god over others, continuing a movement toward monotheism that had begun about 1200 B.C. Marduk, who had been the chief Babylonian god since the time of Hammurabi,

Marduk, the patron deity of Babylon, became the Kassite Empire's supreme god when Babylon became the capital of the empire around 1200 B.C. Marduk was said to have been elevated to the "king of gods" by his fellow deities after proving his supreme status by making a cloth disappear and reappear in their presence.

was credited with creation and was elevated to chief god. A new myth, called the Epic of Creation, described Marduk's creational identity. To commemorate Marduk, the story was read aloud as part of annual celebrations observing the Babylonian New Year. In their readings, the Babylonians related the story of the assembly of gods proclaiming Marduk's primacy among the gods:

> You are the most hounoured one among the great gods,
> Your decree is unequaled, your utterance is Anu . . .
> From this very day your command shall be unalterable,
> To exalt or to bring low, this is verily in your hand,
> What comes forth from your mouth shall come true, your
>   utterance shall not prove false;
> No one among the gods shall overstep your bounds . . .
> We have given you kingship over the whole universe;
> Sit in the Assembly and let your word be supreme![16]

According to the legend, Marduk then passed a test that proved his supreme status, causing a cloth to disappear and reappear in the presence of the gods. In response, "They rejoiced and gave blessing: 'Marduk is king!' Then they added to him the sceptre, the throne, and the *palu* [the insignia of royalty]."[17] Thus, Marduk was seen not only as the leading god, but also as the king of gods, proclaimed and recognized by the other gods as supreme among them. As supreme god, Marduk destroyed all enemy gods and then created the world.

Despite his powers, Marduk proved incapable of protecting the Kassite dynasty forever. In 1157 B.C., a group from what is modern-day southern Iran invaded Babylonia. These invaders, the Elamites, attacked and overran virtually every major Babylonian city. They even captured two of the Babylonians' most prized possessions. One of these was the seven-and-a-half-foot stone monument inscribed with the Code of

Hammurabi. The other was a statue of Marduk. The humiliated Babylonians seemed to face a foe that could not be beaten, but they managed to unite and stand up to the Elamites. A new line of kings was established and began driving the invaders from the land. Nebuchadnezzar I forced what was left of the conquering Elamites out of his empire. He followed up his successes by taking the war into Elamite territory, reclaiming the Code of Hammurabi and the statue of Marduk. Later, another Babylonian king very nearly conquered Assyria, managing to conduct a military campaign deep in Assyrian territory and bringing his forces to within 20 miles of Ashur, Assyria's capital city.

Babylon's rebirth was short-lived, however, and its status as a regional power suffered a slow decay for about four centuries, beginning about 1100 B.C. It is no coincidence that this decline came at the same time the Assyrians were rising to power. Babylonian strength continued to wane until, in the eighth century B.C., Tiglath-Pileser III of Assyria successfully overthrew Babylon's reigning king and assumed control of Mesopotamia.

4

The Assyrian Empire

F ollowing Hammurabi's reign, Indo-European tribes invaded
the region of the eastern Fertile Crescent in waves over
several centuries: the Hyksos from Egypt, the Kassites from
southern Iran, and the Hurrians from Assyria and Palestine.
This period is sometimes referred to as the Middle Ages of
Antiquity, and it lasted until the Assyrians managed to dislodge
other unwelcome invaders around 1400 B.C. Assyria then set
out to expand its territorial holdings to the north.

Assyria is named after its foremost city, Ashur, which lay on
the Upper Tigris River. Situated north of Babylonia, Ashur lay
on the eastern Fertile Crescent's great trade route and found
itself the victim of frequent invasions, from both north and
south. Consequently, the Assyrians fostered a culture of fierceness and developed a reputation for military prowess. This
ferocity, coupled with their location, allowed the Assyrians to
exact tribute from traders passing through their territory.

A FORMIDABLE FORCE

The Assyrians, like the Babylonians, were Semites. They
adopted many aspects of Babylonian culture; the languages
used by both, for example, were virtually identical. Although
the Assyrians generated very little original literature, they did
maintain large libraries filled with Sumerian and Babylonian
writings. They also adopted many Babylonian gods but
predictably viewed their chief god, Ashur, as supreme. From
the Hittites, the Assyrians learned many valuable innovations
and used them to build their militaristic state. These advances
included the use of iron, which they used to make formidable
weapons, and the acquisition of horses, which they used as
part of their cavalry—the first civilization to use horses in
this way. The Assyrians proved to be exceptionally cruel in
warfare. Atrocities were not hidden but glorified, striking
fear in their enemies. Assyrian rulers seemed to enjoy extol-
ling their conquests. An inscription dating from 1241 B.C.,

detailing the victory of Tukulti-Ninurta over Babylon, is typical of Assyrian boasting:

> Trusting in the great gods, my lords, and in Ishtar, the queen of heaven and earth, who went at the head of my army, I forced Kashtiliash of Babylon to join battle with me. I defeated his troops and slaughtered his men. In the middle of the battle, I personally captured Kashtiliash, the Babylonian king. My feet trod on his royal neck, he was my footstool. I brought him captive and bound before the god Ashur, my Lord. All Sumer and Akkad I brought under my sway.[18]

Babylon remained a vassal state to Assyria for six centuries. When the Babylonians finally rose against their oppressors, they exacted an equally severe revenge on the Assyrians, nearly wiping them out.

However, during the six centuries that Assyria controlled the region, its power was unrivalled. As Assyrian power grew, that of the Hittites and Egyptians waned. As a military force, the Assyrians were without equal. Although they continued to wage their campaigns on horseback, they also adopted the Hittite chariot and eventually began to use it as their primary military weapon. Their chariots were pulled by horses rather than the donkeys or oxen used by others who used chariots. In addition, the Assyrians employed an engineering corps, complete with siege towers and battering rams. These weapons of war would not be seen again until the Romans made use of similar equipment while expanding and maintaining their empire. With these military strategies and advances, Assyria grew to be the undisputed ruler of Mesopotamia by the middle of the ninth century B.C.

TIGLATH-PILESER I (r. 1115–1077 B.C.)

The ruler who led Assyria to dominance and notoriety was

Tiglath-Pileser I, who initiated his reign by defeating an Anatolian tribe that endangered Nineveh and the country's trade routes with Asia Minor. Because Assyria relied on these trade routes for its supply of iron, Tiglath-Pileser was determined to protect them. After defeating the Anatolians, Tiglath-Pileser fought and subdued Phoenician cities on the Mediterranean Sea, mountain tribes in Armenia, and Aramaean tribes near the Euphrates. He even captured Babylon but chose to exercise no control over the city. As proficient as he was in war, Tiglath-Pileser seemed equally interested in creating a prosperous kingdom. His reign oversaw the refurbishment of the temple of his god, Ashur, in his capital city (also named Ashur). This renovation included a new roof made of cedar— tribute from coastal cities in Syria and Lebanon. He also added a large library filled with literary works to his new and improved temple. Ziggurats were rehabilitated and rededicated. In Nineveh, new parks, teeming with greenery, were built. They were watered by a canal system that diverted the flow of a tributary of the Tigris River into the city. Other Assyrian cities also underwent beautification projects as Tiglath-Pileser sought to encourage his nation to live "in peaceful habitations."[19]

Perhaps the most lasting legacy of Tiglath-Pileser I is one of cruelty and barbarism. It was under his reign that the Assyrians began to judge their military conquests by the degree to which the vanquished were made to suffer. In an account of the Assyrian conquest over the Anatolians, Tiglath-Pileser boasted:

> With their twenty thousand warriors and their five kings I fought . . . and I defeated them. . . . Their blood I let flow in the valleys and on the high levels of the mountains. I cut off their heads and outside their cities, like heaps of grain, I piled them up. . . . I burned their cities with fire, I demolished them, I cleared them away.[20]

Clearly, Tiglath-Pileser used terror and fear to subdue his rivals. Despite his interest in creating peaceful and beautiful cities for his people, his interest in military success was unabashedly strong. In another inscription, Tiglath-Pileser declared: "Lands, mountains, cities, and princes I have conquered and brought under my yoke. I fought sixty kings and established my invincible power over them. I personally was unequalled in battle, unrivalled in combat." [21]

Despite the fierceness Tiglath-Pileser displayed and the terror he instilled, the Assyrian monarch did not prove to be an able administrator. Although he managed to keep the conquered peoples in check during his lifetime, there was no love lost between the vanquished and their Assyrian overlords. However, as soon as Tiglath-Pileser I died, the vassals rose up against their overlords and nearly a century and a half of almost continuous rebellion followed. During those 150 years, the Assyrian Empire dwindled to a narrow piece of land bordering the Tigris River. Their territory reduced to just 100 miles wide and 50 miles long, the Assyrians were unable to stop marauding tribes from entering and establishing themselves in the region. One of those tribes, the Chaldeans (originally called the Kaldu), would later become the new rulers in Babylon.

ASHURNASIRPAL II (r. 883–859 B.C.)

During the 150 years of revolts that sapped the strength of the empire, a new breed of ruler came to the Assyrian throne, one that sought to aggressively reestablish Assyrian supremacy in the region. The first of these aggressive rulers was Ashurnasirpal II. Some scholars believe that Ashurnasirpal II inherited the best-equipped and most experienced troops in the Near East. With iron-headed battering rams and other siege machinery, and a reorganized army that featured the Assyrian staples of cavalry, charioteers, bowmen, and infantry, Ashurnasirpal II extended Assyria to the Mediterranean Sea. As a symbol of his

Ashurnasirpal II, who was king of Assyria from 883 to 859 B.C., extended the Assyrian Empire westward to the Mediterranean Sea and oversaw the construction of a new capital, Calah, which is known today as Nimrud. This painting by James Fergusson details the newly constructed palaces of Calah.

power over Phoenician cities, Ashurnasirpal washed his weapons in the Mediterranean. Like his predecessors, he worked to reassert control over lost territories. Like the earlier Assyrian kings, Ashurnasirpal made a name for himself by committing brutal atrocities. He recounted the violence meted out against some of his foes:

> I built a pillar over against his city gate, and I flayed all the chief men . . . and I covered the pillar with their skins; some I walled up within the pillar, some I impaled upon the pillar on stakes . . . and I cut off the limbs of the officers. . . . Many captives from among them I burned with fire. . . . From some I cut off their hands and their fingers, and from others I cut off their noses, their ears . . . of many I put out the eyes. . . . Their young men and maidens I burned in the fire.[22]

While he persisted in promoting the savagery and viciousness upon which the Assyrian Empire was built, Ashurnasirpal II also oversaw the construction of a new capital city called Calah, which is present-day Nimrud. There he built a massive and beautiful palace that covered six acres. It was lavishly decorated and contained many rooms. It was, in Ashurnasirpal's words:

> A palace of cedar, cypress, juniper, boxwood, mulberry, pistachio-wood, and tamarisk, for my royal dwelling and for my lordly pleasure for all time I founded therein. Beasts of the mountains and of the seas of white limestone and alabaster I fashioned, and set them up in its gates. I made it suitable, I made it glorious.... Door-leaves of cedar, cypress, juniper, and mulberry I hung in the gates thereof; and silver, gold, tin, bronze, and iron, the spoil of my hand from the lands which I had brought under my sway, in great quantities I took and I placed therein.[23]

Ashurnasirpal's successors continued to extend Assyrian territory through military conquest. King Tiglath-Pileser III (r. 745–727 B.C.) seized Damascus and later Assyrian kings would conquer Israel, Sidon, Phoenicia, and Egypt. To facilitate conquests and maintain control over their growing list of vanquished foes, the Assyrians constructed roads throughout their empire. These same roads were utilized when they established a well-planned and orderly system of mail delivery, which enabled the king to keep in close, albeit indirect, touch with the officials who ruled in his stead in conquered territories.

SARGON II (r. 721–705 B.C.)

Sargon II, not to be confused with the Akkadian who successfully conquered the Sumerian cities some 1,600 years earlier, assumed the Assyrian throne in 721 B.C. By this time, the empire was filled with unrest, and Sargon turned his attention to restoring order and control over Assyria's rebellious provinces. Although he managed to extend the boundaries of the empire, most of his time and energies were occupied with stifling insurgencies.

Sargon did manage to conquer Israel, placing it under Assyrian control. Consistent with Assyrian custom, Sargon carried off some 30,000 Israelites into captivity. It was during this Assyrian conquest that the ten northern tribes of Israel became the Ten Lost Tribes of Israel.

Sargon, however, had other interests that mirrored those of his predecessors. Late in his reign, Sargon decided to abandon Calah and build his own capital city. He named his new capital Dur-Sharrukin (modern-day Khorsabad) and began to construct a palace that would surpass all before it in lavishness and immensity. Within a decade, his palace was more impressive than Ashurnasirpal's palace in Calah. The massive building, situated north of Nineveh, occupied some 25 acres and included nearly 1,000 rooms. Nearby, Sargon erected a massive temple, a ziggurat that climbed seven stories into the sky. At its gates were colossal stone statues of bulls with human heads. Inside the palace, the walls were decorated with alabaster and limestone relief that extolled the accomplishments of Sargon and his people. Sargon, however, had little time to take pleasure in his great palace—he died in battle not long after its completion and was succeeded by his son, Sennacherib.

SENNACHERIB (r. 705–681 B.C.)

Sennacherib's capital city was Nineveh and there the new ruler built three different palaces, each splendid and lavishly decorated. Whereas the Babylonians had decorated their walls with variously colored glazed bricks, the Assyrians used carved slabs of alabaster or limestone. Surviving examples include enormous winged bulls or lions with human heads, standing at the entrances to their temples and palaces.

Like other Assyrian rulers, however, Sennacherib is best remembered for his ruthlessness. It was under his reign that Assyria captured Palestine and forced King Hezekiah to pay tribute to Nineveh. Sennacherib also subjugated Sidon and Phoenicia and brutally repressed a Babylonian revolt by completely destroying the city of Babylon. Sennacherib described the devastation he brought on the city:

> With [the corpses of it inhabitants] I filled the city squares. . . . The city and houses, from its foundation to its top, I destroyed, I devastated, I burned with fire. The wall and outer wall, temples and gods, temple-towers of brick and earth, as many as there were, I razed. . . . Through the midst of that city I dug canals [from the Euphrates River], I flooded its site with water. . . . That in days to come the site of that city, and [its] temples and gods, might not be recognized. I dissolved it in water . . . annihilated it, making it like a meadow.[24]

The Euphrates—which like the Tigris is virtually synonymous with life because of its waters—was thus turned into a weapon of violence, temporarily aiding in erasing Babylon from the region. The obliteration was not permanent: Babylon was to rise for one more period of dynastic supremacy. As for Sennacherib, he was accorded the same consideration he had shown the ancient city of Babylon. His own sons brutally murdered him eight years after he triumphed over the Babylonian capital.

ESARHADDON (r. 680–669 B.C.)

After his murder, Sennacherib's sons vied for control of the throne, and Esarhaddon eventually won out over his brothers.

Sennacherib, the ruthless Assyrian king who reigned from 705 to 681 B.C., sacked a number of cities in Judah but was unable to capture Jerusalem, the kingdom's capital. An account of Sennacherib's failure to capture Jerusalem is detailed in Isaiah 36–37 in the Bible.

He only ruled for 11 years, but they were 11 glorious years for the Assyrian Empire. Even given the brief length of his reign, Esarhaddon may very well be the most noteworthy king of Assyria. He rebuilt the city of Babylon, which his father Sennacherib had razed. Unlike earlier rulers, he used both the sword and diplomacy to secure peace along Assyria's borders. Once he had forged treaties with those most likely to endanger the peace, Esarhaddon undertook a massive invasion of Egypt in 671 B.C. In less than a month, Esarhaddon brought Egypt to its knees. He captured the northern Egyptian capital of Memphis after a siege that lasted only a day and a half. Egypt submitted to Assyrian power and remained a vassal of the great power for 16 years. Ruling Assyria now that it reached its largest size, Esarhaddon claimed, "I am powerful, I am all-powerful. . . . I am without an equal among all kings."[25] When Esarhaddon died, his heir, Ashurbanipal, inherited an empire stretching over 1,000 miles—from Egypt to the Caucasus Mountains in Armenia.

ASHURBANIPAL (r. 668–627 B.C.)

Ashurbanipal's Assyria was simply too large to maintain. The empire had overextended its resources, straining its ability to govern without constantly being at war. Despite the fear vassal states had of losing a war to the Assyrians, the constant demands for tribute and Assyrian brutality often led to widespread revolts throughout the empire. Ashurbanipal proved to be the last Assyrian king capable of suppressing these revolts. After Ashurbanipal, the Assyrian capital itself would be unable to withstand the onslaught of the pent-up anger and resentment toward past acts of Assyrian savagery.

In 626 B.C., Ashurbanipal died. Soon after, the Medes and the Babylonians formed an alliance and rose against the Assyrians. Their combined forces destroyed Nineveh in 612 B.C. All that could not be carried off was burned. The destruction was so complete that Herodotus, who traveled through the region just 150 years after Nineveh's defeat, failed to even notice or record seeing the site. In fact, Nineveh was so thoroughly obliterated that the location of the city was lost until it was finally rediscovered in the nineteenth century.

Three years after Nineveh's annihilation, the breakdown of the Assyrian Empire was complete. The remaining Assyrian forces and their Egyptian allies were soundly defeated by the Chaldeans. One of the lesser-known Semitic peoples, the Chaldeans had become the ruling class of a new and restored Chaldean-Babylonian Empire.

Following the collapse of the Assyrian Empire, Babylon experienced some seventy years of peace and autonomy. The Chaldeans, like the Kassites before them, adopted much of Babylonian culture; in essence, they became Babylonians. They purposely chose to make Babylon their capital, and Babylon retained its role as the cultural and educational center of the region despite persistent meddling, control, and even destruction by an assortment of marauding and conquering tribes. The successful rebirth of the Babylonian Empire can be attributed to the manifold achievements of Nebuchadnezzar II.

NEBUCHADNEZZAR II (r. 605–561 B.C.)

Nebuchadnezzar II rose to power and restored the strength and wealth of old Babylon as Assyrian power and influence deteriorated. Nebuchadnezzar is probably most well known for his campaign against Jerusalem, during which the city and the Hebrew temple were destroyed. The subsequent detention of the Hebrew people is known as the Babylonian Captivity and is recorded in the Old Testament.

There is, however, more to the reputation of Nebuchadnezzar II than conquest. It was under his rule that Babylon became one of the most impressive cities in the world. The Babylon he inherited stood on the west bank of the Euphrates. The great king expanded the city walls to cross the river and connected the two sections with a large stone bridge, thus ensuring a reliable water source for the city—even if it was under siege. He also constructed immense palaces and temples for his refurbished and spacious city. Undoubtedly the most famous of Nebuchadnezzar's architectural achievements was the celebrated and prominent Hanging Gardens, acclaimed by the Greeks as one of the Seven Wonders of the Ancient World.

Other architectural feats included the Gate of Ishtar and numerous ziggurats. The Gate of Ishtar reached over Procession Street, where the Temple of Marduk was located. Near the temple dedicated to Babylon's chief god was a grand ziggurat, complete with seven distinct stories, each elevated level recessed from the one below. A sloping ramp spiraled its way around the building to the top. According to Herodotus, the famous Greek historian, each of the seven receding levels was painted a different color: white, black, purple, blue, orange, silver, and gold. Some, including Herodotus, believed that this was the original Tower of Babel described in Genesis. Even if this ziggurat is indeed the Tower of Babel, it is simply one of many man-made holy mountains located in and near Babylon. (For additional information on this holy structure, enter "bible tower of babel" into any search engine and browse the many sites listed.)

THE PERSIANS AND THE GREEKS

Throughout Nebuchadnezzar's reign, Babylon maintained its sovereignty and supremacy in the region. In 539 B.C., however, Persian forces, led by Cyrus the Great, conquered the city. Surprisingly, Babylon retained its role as a cultural and trade center. The city was still reasonably affluent when invading Greeks arrived with Alexander the Great two centuries later. Alexander's father Philip was king of Macedon and had united Greece during his reign. Following Philip's death, the young Alexander conquered much of the ancient Near East, including the Persian Empire. Eventually, the young Macedonian succeeded in extending his territory all the way to the Indus River. When Alexander conquered the Persians, he made Nebuchadnezzar's palace his own. Following Alexander's

THE HANGING GARDENS OF BABYLON

One of the Seven Wonders of the Ancient World, the Hanging Gardens of Babylon were located within the royal palace. They were called "hanging" because they were "up in the air," possibly rising to a height of 75 feet.* The hanging gardens were planted on roofs, on a series of terraces that lined each level of the palace ziggurats. Water pumped from the nearby Euphrates River was used to irrigate the gardens. According to tradition, the gardens were built by one of two Babylonian rulers. Some believe they were the work of Queen Sammuramat (called Semiramis in Greek and recognized as the mother of King Adad-Nirari III of Assyria). Other scholars have argued that Semiramis is nothing more than a mythical figure. Most scholars who believe in the existence of the hanging gardens give credit to King Nebuchadnezzar II for creating the environmental wonder. It is said that King Nebuchadnezzar had the gardens constructed to soothe his wife, the Median princess Amytis, who was the daughter of Cyaxares and who missed the indigenous foliage and mountains of her native land.

The hanging gardens, which flourished in the midst of desert land, must have been an impressive sight to visitors of the great city. In fact, they were described often and in great detail by authors of the ancient world, giving us some idea of what they might have looked like:

> The terraces were roofed with stone balconies on which were layered various materials, such as reeds, bitumen, and lead, so that the irrigation water would not seep through the terraces. Although no certain traces of the Hanging Gardens have been found, German archaeologist Robert Koldewey did uncover an unusual series of foundation chambers and

death in 323 B.C., Seleucus I Nicator succeeded him to the throne of the eastern portions of the Greek Empire. Seleucus built a new capital city, Seleucia, on the Tigris, in large part because the deeper waterway allowed for better navigation than did the Euphrates.

For Babylon, it was the beginning of a slow decline. The city quickly lost its population, most of which relocated to vaults in the northeastern corner of the palace at Babylon. A well in one of these vaults may have been used in conjunction with a chain pump and thus was perhaps part of the substructure of the once towering Hanging Gardens.**

Koldewey himself wrote that he had uncovered a rather unique well. His description includes specific mention of technology that may have served to provide water for the gardens. The well was, according to Koldewey:

A well that differs from all other wells known in Babylon or elsewhere in the ancient world. It has three shafts placed close to each other, a square one in the [center], and oblong ones on each side, an arrangement for which I can see no other explanation than a mechanical hydraulic stood here, which worked on the same principle as our chain pump. . . . This contrivance . . . would provide a continuous flow of water.***

Other evidence that suggests these might be the ruins of the famous architectural wonder can be found in Koldewey's description of the building, which was constructed of hewn stone, not baked or dried mud bricks. Archaeological digs have uncovered portions of the structure that were made of hewn stone, further bolstering Koldewey's claims.

* "Hanging Gardens of Babylon," *Encyclopedia Britannica*, 15th ed., 888.

** Ibid.

*** J.A. Brendon, "The Hanging Gardens of Babylon," in Sir J.A. Hammerton, ed., *Wonders of the Past*, vol. 1 (New York: Wise and Company, 1948), 608.

Seleucia. The vacated buildings and city walls became collection sites for builders seeking bricks. Today, all that remains of the once great and proud city of Babylon are ruins located near the modern Iraqi town of Al Hillah.

5

Persians, Greeks, Muslims, Mongols, and Turks

Mesopotamia was a region that seemed to invite invaders, and much of its history involves the story of each new rising empire marching into the region and placing Mesopotamia's inhabitants under its control. All of these invasions and conquering peoples left their mark, merging and integrating parts of their cultures into the surviving culture of the land between the rivers. The successive waves of Persians, Greeks, Muslims, Mongols, and Turks helped shape modern Mesopotamian culture. Their collective and respective influence is seen in the administration of government, respect for strong rulers, adherence to Islamic beliefs, and a myriad of other political and cultural developments. Historian Norman F. Cantor described Mesopotamia's early history:

> The history of the Tigris-Euphrates valley was shaped by a series of invasions from the north. As Sumerians, Chaldeans, Assyrians, and Babylonians succeeded one another, the structure of severely class-ridden societies and agriculture-based economies did not change. The series of invasions and conquests ended around 500 B.C. with Iraq absorbed into the expanding Iranian (Persian) empire to the east.[26]

MEDES AND PERSIANS

The Persians were descended from a group of nomads who arrived in the Middle East from Central Asia around 1000 B.C. They called themselves Irani (or Aryans) and their adopted home Iran. Greeks called them "Persians" after the name of their province, Pars, or their capital, Persis. Like their close relatives, the Medes, the Persians looked and behaved as if they were Semitic, but their languages were Indo-Iranian. (Languages of this group are more closely related to modern European languages than to the Semitic group of languages.)

The Medes had already been in Mesopotamia for some time, but scholars are unsure when they first arrived. Assyrian texts from the ninth century B.C. make the first historical mention of the Medes, but because few physical objects from their culture have survived, scholars know very little about their way of life. What is known is that the Medes and Persians did share some of the same characteristics. Both the Medes and the Persians worshiped various nature gods, but the teachings of Zoroaster in the sixth century B.C., which emphasized the forces of light and darkness, led to the adoption of Zoroastrianism as the state religion in Persia.

Over several generations, the Medes developed into a mighty force that began to assert itself in the region. The ancient Greek historian Herodotus, who wrote one of the first narrative histories of the ancient world, records that the Median King Phraortes, while laying siege to Nineveh, was killed by the Scythians. His son, Cyaxares (r. 625–585 B.C.), was forced to endure the rule of the Scythians until he killed their leaders at a great banquet. Historians disagree with Herodotus that Phraortes united the Medes, contending that it was Cyaxares who brought the tribes together to fight the Assyrians. Cyaxares reorganized his forces, separating his bowmen, cavalry, and spearmen, as well as improving weaponry, for each component of his army. Under Cyaxares, the Medes grew in strength and seized Ashur, located on the Tigris River, in 614 B.C. In 612 B.C., the forces of Cyaxares successfully attacked and destroyed the Assyrian capital of Nineveh, which also lay on the Tigris River.

The Medes then extended their control eastward throughout the region (they eventually took control over much of modern-day Iran and parts of Armenia) and fought with the Babylonians in their campaign against the Assyrians between 612 and 609 B.C. The Medes and the Babylonians then split Assyria between them. By 600 B.C., the Medes had built an extensive empire that enveloped Mesopotamia and included Assyrians in the west and Persians in the east. It seemed that the kingdom led by Cyaxares was destined for greatness; however, the great king died in 585 B.C. Within a generation, the Medes fell to the founder of the Achaemenid dynasty, Persia's King Cyrus the Great. Because the Medes and Persians shared many cultural traits and customs, it is thus not surprising that the Medes were simply absorbed into the Persian Empire. In fact, this empire is often called the Medo-Persian Empire; its people are called the Medo-Persians, reflecting the extent to which the Medes were integrated into the Persian political and cultural fold.

The Achaemenid dynasty began with the ascension of Cyrus to the throne in 559 B.C. and would last until Alexander the Great arrived with his conquering Greek forces in 330 B.C. Some historians date the Achaemenid era, which saw the growth and dominance of Persia as a world power, 10 years later, when Cyrus unseated Astyages from the Median throne. Either way, it was Cyrus who extended Persian holdings from Asia Minor and Palestine in the west to Persia (Iran) in the east, including the earlier Assyrian and Babylonian Empires—Babylon having surrendered to Cyrus in 538 B.C. with virtually no resistance. Cyrus later expanded his empire to India, but he was killed while fighting against nomads in the East in 529 B.C. Seven years later, Darius the Great (or Darius I), who ruled from 522 to 486 B.C., ascended to the throne and continued the expansion of the empire founded by Cyrus.

DARIUS I, XERXES, AND DARIUS III

The Persian Empire prospered under Darius I. Perhaps his most impressive achievement was his efficient administration of his government. The empire was divided into 20 provinces called satrapies. A satrap, who was appointed by the king, governed each satrapy. Satraps were responsible for collecting the annual tribute from their provinces for the king. Other royally appointed officials, loosely known as the "king's eyes," regularly visited the satrapies and reported directly to the king. This allowed the king to keep a close watch over his vast empire. Each satrapy was required to provide soldiers for the Persian army, and some of the more sea-faring provinces (Egypt, Greek colonies in Asia Minor, and Phoenicia) even furnished ships and sailors. This well-organized system proved extremely effective in helping to increase the Persian monarch's wealth. Vast amounts of riches poured into the royal treasuries, the most famous of which was housed in Susa. Darius wisely used this wealth to encourage trade and commerce within the empire. Coins were minted from gold, and a standardized system of weights and measure and coinage was introduced. Darius even had a canal dug that connected the Nile River with the Red Sea. Imperial highways were constructed, linking many of the empire's major cities. These roads also served to remind satraps that the king's armies could come to enforce collection of tribute and Medo-Persian laws.

Despite his achievements, Darius spent much of his reign stifling revolts and uprisings throughout the empire. Darius, for example, launched an expedition against the Greek city-state of Athens for its role in aiding a revolt of the Greek cities in Asia Minor in 500 B.C. His massive expedition was repelled at the battle of Marathon. Darius planned to lead another campaign against the Greeks but died in 486 B.C. before plans for the expedition could be realized. He was succeeded by his son Xerxes, who ruled from 486 to 465 B.C. (For additional information on this famous battle, enter "Battle of Marathon" into any search engine and browse the many sites listed.)

Xerxes was a harsh and oppressive ruler who demanded obedience and loyalty from his subjects. After inheriting the throne, Xerxes was forced to suppress revolts in Egypt and Babylon before assembling a massive army with which he intended to crush the Greeks. For a time, it appeared that Xerxes would conquer the many Greek city-states, but after being defeated at the battles of Salamis and Plataea, he was forced

This mosaic, currently displayed at the National Museum of Naples (Italy), portrays Darius III in his chariot during the battle of Issus (near present-day Iskenderun, Turkey) in 333 B.C. Darius III was the last ruler of the Persian Empire and despite outnumbering Alexander the Great's Macedonian and Greek troops nearly four to one, the Persians were defeated in the battle.

to withdraw his forces to Asia Minor. It would take another 125 years before the Greeks would reciprocate and invade the Persian Empire, but the beginning of the Persian decline was initiated by the setbacks suffered by Xerxes at the hands of the Greek city-states. Indeed, much of the remaining history of the independent Persian Empire is one of intrigue, assassinations, and tax revolts that dominated the government's attention.

After a series of tyrannical kings, some of whom were poisoned or otherwise murdered, Darius III became the last Persian to rule the empire. It was Darius III who was forced to face

Alexander the Great as the Macedonian led his mighty Greek army into the heart of the Persian Empire. Darius was overwhelmingly defeated at the battle of Issus in 333 B.C., but he managed to escape and raise another army. Having taken the western half of the Persian Empire, which included Mesopotamia, Alexander set his sights on the rest of the spoils. In 331 B.C., he met and again defeated Darius at the battle of Arbela, and Darius again fled from the battlefield. In 330 B.C., one of his own men assassinated him, effectively ending the Persian Empire.

Alexander retained control of Persia, but he died in 323 B.C., leaving his empire to be divided among his generals. One of them, Seleucus, claimed Babylon and established the Seleucid dynasty, which also ruled over Persia until 247 B.C. That year, Parthia, one of the provinces under Seleucid rule, successfully rebelled against the Seleucids and united Persia under its own rule. The Parthian kingdom stretched from the Bolan Pass, in present-day Pakistan, westward to the Euphrates River. The Parthians, a nomadic people, managed to maintain independence for some 300 hundred years.

THE GREEKS

The Greek invasion impacted the Tigris and Euphrates plains, as the victors brought with them new customs and beliefs. With the arrival of the Greeks, Mesopotamia was introduced to a new set of influences that left a lasting impression on the region. Some scholars even view the conquest and influence of Greek culture under Alexander the Great as the most significant stage in Mesopotamian history. Historian George Roux compared it to the Renaissance of sixteenth-century Europe. Roux wrote:

> The new world heralded by Alexander was a fast changing world marked by extensive commercial intercourse, bursting with curiosity, eager to re-appraise most of its religious,

CRACKING THE CUNEIFORM CODE

Although tens of thousands of cuneiform tablets were recovered from various sites throughout Mesopotamia beginning in the eighteenth century, scholars were at a loss as to how to translate them. The wedge-shaped markings appeared to be anything but random, but they were unlike any known language and baffled the experts who spent years trying to decipher them. Several individuals and teams of specialists raced to be the first to successfully crack the code that would enable the reading of ancient stone inscriptions and clay tablets.

In 1756, a Danish expedition, led by a German named Carsten Niebuhr, made copies of inscriptions at the ruins of a Persian palace at Persepolis (in present-day Iran). These inscriptions were published in 1772, providing the initial spark for a series of attempts to understand the ancient language of the Sumerians. Niebuhr discovered that the inscriptions were in three different languages, each of which used cuneiform script. The inscriptions did not include enough of two of the languages to enable Niebuhr to decipher them, but the third was soon determined to be Old Persian. Old Persian was the language used approximately 500–300 B.C. in what is now Iran.

Once the third language had been identified as Old Persian, others began to provide additional clues to solve the mystery. The most significant of these was a high school teacher from Germany, Georg Friedrich Grotefend, who first grew interested in the script in 1802. His knowledge of Greek texts—which were used by later Persians—in which predictable patterns were followed, enabled Grotefend to identify certain words in cuneiform. For instance, a typical inscription would read: "X, great king, king of kings, son of Y, great king, king of kings, son of Z, et cetera.*

From this pattern, Grotefend was able to work out a formula. He found that if the name of one king in a series of three could be read, then the identities of the other kings could be translated as well. Applying his formula to the names of several of the more famous son-father-grandfather genealogies from Persian history, Grotefend deduced that the Persepolis inscription read, "Xerxes, great king, king of kings, son of Darius, great king, king of kings, son of Hystapes."**

Thus, Grotefend was the first to successfully translate a cuneiform inscription. He also denoted and identified phonetic values with each Old Persian symbol, paving the way for future decipherers. Unfortunately, the academic community considered Grotefend an amateur (he had begun his work after making a bet) and did not accept his findings. Furthermore, although Grotefend's decipherment did advance the study of cuneiform, it had decoded only one of at least three languages that used the ancient script.

The next most notable linguist to tackle part of the cuneiform puzzle was Henry Creswicke Rawlinson, a soldier who first traveled east as a member of Great Britain's Indian Army. In 1835, Rawlinson was posted to Persia. He learned of some ancient rock carvings of King Darius near a small town called Behistun. There were indeed carvings at the site, but Rawlinson also found some 1,200 lines of cuneiform text. Like the inscriptions at Persepolis, they were written in three different languages. There was another major impediment to reading and recording the inscriptions— they were located on a cliff face, more than 300 feet high. Rawlinson tried using a telescope to record the inscriptions, but the job proved too difficult. For several years, Rawlinson returned to the site to make copies of the inscriptions for decipherment. Using a ladder, he scaled the cliff face. He then repositioned the ladder on a two-foot ledge at the base of the inscription. In order to read the uppermost sections, Rawlinson balanced himself on the top rung of his ladder, recording the symbols in a notebook. Part of the ledge was missing and Rawlinson was forced to use his ladder as a bridge. He survived a scare when one side of the ladder slipped and nearly dumped him to the canyon floor. Later, he claimed, "The interest of the occupation did away with any sense of danger."***

The last inscription was carved in rock above the middle inscription, which later proved to be Elamite. It seemed to be inaccessible even to local mountain climbers, and Rawlinson believed the carvings to be beyond his reach. Fortunately, a young Kurdish boy volunteered to help Rawlinson and thanks to some skillful climbing and ingenuity, the boy was able to make a paper caste of the inscription.

Rawlinson, who had been appointed British resident to Baghdad in December 1843, then set about trying to decipher the inscriptions. His

moral, scientific and artistic values. There was no room in such a world for a literature which none but a few scholars could read, for an art which drew its inspiration from outdated ideals and models, for a science which evaded rational explanations, for a religion which did not admit summer home in Baghdad, situated near the river, was "a curious feat of local engineering: a waterwheel, turned by the onrushing waters of the Tigris, poured a continuous stream of fresh water over the roof of the library. The temperature within the study hovered at a relatively cool 90 degrees Fahrenheit. Outside the thermometer soared to 120."[+]

Rawlinson also kept some rather exotic animals as pets, including a mongoose, a black panther, and a full-grown Mesopotamian lioness. It was here amidst his unusual animals in his water-cooled study that he made some startling discoveries. The Behistun inscriptions were in three languages: Old Persian, Elamite, and Akkadian. Rawlinson effectively cracked the cuneiform code and published his findings in 1851.

Others soon embarked on similar translation projects and published their work, but many in the European academic community doubted that anyone could actually read the ancient cuneiform script. In 1857, the Royal Asiatic Society conducted a test with four of the most prominent translators: Rawlinson, Edward Hicks, Jules Opert, and William Henry Fox Talbot. Rubbings from a near-perfect clay cylinder, which had been uncovered in 1853, put the translators to the test.

The four independent translations were not identical, but each of the translators demonstrated that he could read the ancient script. The secrets of the cuneiform code were now exposed to research and study, and the Sumerian culture again came to life as scholars and students rediscovered the ancient people through their peculiar writing.

* James Wellard, *Babylon* (New York: Saturday Review Press, 1972), 66.

** Ibid.

*** *Sumer: Cities of Eden* (Alexandria, Va.: Time-Life Books, 1993), 20.

+ Arnold C. Brackman, *The Luck of Nineveh: Archaeology's Great Adventure* (New York: McGraw-Hill, 1978), 132.

skepticism. The Mesopotamian civilization, like its Egyptian counterpart, was condemned. If it were permissible to enclose a highly complex phenomenon into one single and necessarily inaccurate formula, one could say that it died of old age.[27]

Whether it died of old age or conquest, there is no disputing that Mesopotamian culture gradually fell under the sway of the appealing Hellenistic way of life brought by the Greeks. One historian described the subtle influence of Greek civilization:

> Alexander's entrance into Babylonia in 331 B.C. . . . marks another epoch in the world's history. Even after Alexander, the religious and social life of Babylonia goes on unchanged to outward appearances, but the contact with Greek civilization destroyed what little vitality had survived the impetus of the new force represented by Persia and Zoroastrianism. Up to within a few decades of the Christian era, the Babylonian language and script continued in use, but Greek ideas and Greek usages had made their way not only into the government of the country but also into the life of the people.[28]

As for Babylon, the hopes and dreams of resurrecting itself yet again died with Alexander the Great in 323 B.C. The city never again rose to prominence. Instead, it slowly became absorbed into Greek culture and, later, into the cultures of the competing powers that came to control Mesopotamia over the subsequent centuries.

PARTHIA AND ROME

The Parthians, or the later Persians, were the first of several powers to dominate Mesopotamia after the Greek conquest. Unfortunately, historians know little of the Parthians because few written sources remain from their era. What is known is that the Parthians, led by Arsaces, successfully revolted against the Seleucids in 247 B.C. and established a rule that would last through the first quarter of the third century A.D. In 211 B.C., Parthia's King Artabanus I added the Tigris-Euphrates River valley to Parthian holdings. The Parthians minted coins and proved capable of defending themselves against the encroachments of the Roman Empire. The two powers met diplomatically in 96 B.C., but the issue of territorial boundaries was far from settled. Unable to successfully negotiate a treaty, the two finally agreed to recognize the Euphrates as a boundary in 92 B.C. When Parthia later suffered from internal strife, Rome attempted to take advantage of the opportunity. The Roman general Crassus boasted in 54 B.C. that he would defeat Parthia and add its lands to the Roman Empire. Instead, Crassus was defeated in battle the next year and beheaded by the Parthians. Twenty years later, a Parthian victory over Roman troops in Armenia forced Rome to end its claims to any lands east of the Euphrates. Later Roman attempts to conquer Parthia eventually weakened the empire, contributing to its downfall. The downfall, however, primarily came from within the empire—the Parthians were overthrown by one of their own provinces. This upstart province, ruled by Ardashir I, established the Sassanid dynasty in A.D. 224.

The Sassanid dynasty derives its name from Sassan, from whom Ardashir descended. During the Sassanid period, war with Rome was nearly constant as the empire to the west sought to add Persia to its domain. After Christianity was legalized and adopted by the Roman Empire in the fourth century A.D., Sassanid persecution of Christians inevitably led to conflict with the Church in Constantinople. Under Sassanid rule, Zoroastrianism was reintroduced as the official state religion, and they extended their influence by conquering both Syria and Armenia. Little evidence remains to reveal the culture or daily life of the Sassanids, but Sassanid rule lasted until 640, when the Arabs wrested control of their lands and introduced a new and powerful force to the region: Islam.

ISLAM

The introduction of Islam into Mesopotamia and its eventual adoption there would reshape some of the cultural practices of the region's population. The Sassanid remnants of the Persian Empire proved unable to withstand the onslaught of the caliphates of the Islamic dynasties, which would gain and then retain their hold in the region for the next six centuries.

Muhammad, the founder of Islam, was born about A.D. 570 in the city of Mecca in what is now Saudi Arabia. Very little is known about his early life. He was born into a poor clan, and his father died before he was born, making it impossible for Muhammad to inherit his father's property. Muhammad was orphaned at the age of six and raised by an uncle. As a young man, he successfully engaged in the caravan trade, working for a wealthy widow whom he later married. In A.D. 610, Muhammad began preaching a new religion in Mecca, a religion that recognized a single god: Allah. Although his message was initially reserved for his closest family, he began to broaden his audience and preach publicly in 617. His teachings were later written down in the Qur'an (or Recitation).

Muhammad claimed to be a messenger or prophet of Allah. Although he gained many followers in Mecca, his teachings drew strong opposition. Muhammad preached that those with means must help the poor. This did little to endear him to the city's wealthy clans. Furthermore, Muhammad challenged traditional beliefs and customs. Recognizing just one god—Allah—Muhammad denounced the locally accepted worship of the Black Stone. Believed to be a meteorite, the stone was worshipped as a god until Muhammad put a stop to the practice. Muhammad did, however, incorporate the Black Stone into Islamic beliefs, teaching that the stone fell from heaven at the feet of Adam and was later rediscovered by Abraham. (Today, the Black Stone is housed in the Kaaba, or House of Allah, in Mecca. It is the holiest Muslim site.) From the start, the opposition applied some pressure but mostly waited for the right opportunity to deal decisively with Muhammad and his teachings.

The opportunity came with the death of Muhammad's uncle. The new clan leader removed Muhammad from the protection of the clan, which meant that the law no longer offered him any protection. In 622, Muhammad and his followers fled to the rival city of Medina. This flight is known as the *Hijira* and marks the beginning of the Muslim calendar. In Medina, Muhammad continued to teach his new religion. After a time, Muhammad and his followers began raiding Meccan trading caravans. The raids escalated until open conflict erupted in 624 at Badr. After several other battles, Meccan forces actually laid siege to Medina, but because they were inexperienced with such tactics, the operation lasted only a day. The failure to seize Medina became the turning point for allies of Mecca, many of whom (such as the Persians and southern Arabs) decided not to participate in the conflict. Muhammad's strength gradually grew, and in 630, he returned to Mecca as a conquering hero. Muhammad then set out to conquer local tribes, forming alliances with them. The vanquished sealed these alliances by accepting Islam as their religion and formed the nucleus of the growing religion. Muhammad died in 632, but the faith he had founded was already spreading throughout the Arab world.

After Muhammad's death, the question of succession immediately became a heated issue. Muhammad's successors were *caliphs* (a term that means "successor to the Prophet"). For a time, there were two rivals who claimed to be legitimate leaders. The two claimants to succeed Muhammad were related by marriage—one was Muhammad's father-in-law and the other his son-in-law. The succession issue centered on whether the position of caliph should be determined by election or through heredity. The two sides to this debate paved the way for two different Islamic ruling dynasties in Mesopotamia: the Umayyad and the Abbasid. The Umayyad believed in the elected succession of the caliph and opposed Ali, Muhammad's son-in-law. (Ali's successors were called *Imams* or spiritual leaders.) Another issue involved whether or not non-Arab Muslims could hold leadership positions. Since the inhabitants of Mesopotamia were not Arabs, they predictably followed the Ali faction, which recognized individuals based on their faith instead of their ethnicity.

The early caliphs, especially Omar, who was the second caliph to follow Muhammad, enjoyed widespread military successes. By the time Omar died in 643—just 11 years after Muhammad —the Muslims had reached western India. Wherever Muslim forces went, they took Islam with them. The conflict within Islam, however, intensified after the death of the last of the elected "patriarchal caliphs" in 656. After the last hereditary caliph of the Ali line died, the followers of Ali became identified as Shiite Muslims, one of two major branches of Islam that exist to this day. (The other major branch is Sunni.)

THE UMAYYAD DYNASTY

Under the Umayyad dynasty, which lasted until 750, the Muslim Empire continued to grow, stretching westward across North Africa to Spain and eastward to the Indus River. Interestingly, the means by which the Umayyad selected caliphs more closely resembled a hereditary monarchy than the conferring of power by election in a spiritual or tribal setting. The caliph named his successor (usually, his son) and a group of the most powerful tribal leaders would officially recognize him as the new caliph. Essentially, this group "elected" the caliph after he had been chosen by his predecessor. For this reason, Islamic historians often do not recognize the Umayyad dynasty as a caliphate; instead, they label it a kingdom.

Another way in which the Umayyad dynasty distinguished itself was its decidedly secular bent. The Umayyad clan traced its roots to Mecca, to one of the wealthy clans who initially opposed Muhammad. Due to their secularism, many devout Muslims never really embraced their leadership, but it is likely that this secular leaning helped the Umayyad to build an efficient and enduring governmental structure that would long outlive the dynasty. One caliph, for example, implemented the Byzantine (essentially Roman) model of finance and administration in the capital of Damascus.

One element that promoted Umayyad governmental success was the way in which Umayyad caliphs distinguished themselves from ordinary citizens. Whereas Muhammad and the patriarchal caliphs had lived modestly, the Umayyad caliphs lived as aristocrats. Like the leaders of surrounding countries, they created courts, dressed elegantly, accumulated wealth, and engaged in pomp and circumstance. These practices, of course, further divided the caliphs from the common people and fostered a resentment of the Umayyad rulers. Nevertheless, Islamic culture flourished under the Umayyad. The great mosque in Damascus, an excellent example of Muslim architecture, was built; art was produced; and Muslim writers began producing literary works.

One practice initiated by Umayyad rulers that had far-reaching implications was their treatment of nonbelievers in conquered territory. Nonbelievers were not forced to convert to Islam, but they were required to pay an additional tax. Consequently, many non-Arabs began to convert to Islam, a practice that threatened the Arab nature of the religion. Nowhere was this tension more evident than in the spoken and written language of Islam. As the number of Coptic speaking (Egyptians) and Persian speaking Muslims increased, the Umayyad instituted Arabic as the official language of the empire. Since Mesopotamian residents were of non-Arab descent, their conversion to Islam brought them limited acceptance into Umayyad society.

THE ABBASID DYNASTY

The power base that helped establish the Abbasid caliphate included two groups within the Muslim community that had

The golden dome of the Shrine of Askari, in Samarra, Iraq, was built during the first half of the Abbasid dynasty (A.D. 750–1258). The Abbasids promoted the revival of literary and philosophical works of both Greek and Indian writers, and were responsible for spreading these classic beliefs to the West.

been shut out under the Umayyad: Shiites and non-Arabic Muslims. Both of these groups opposed the Umayyad because of the secularism in their administration of the empire. The Abbasids derive their name from al-Abbas, Muhammad's paternal uncle and staunch defender. No later than 718 did a great-grandson of al-Abbas, Muhammad ibn Ali, begin to build support in Persia for regaining the caliphate for the Prophet's family. Abbasid success, however, relied upon "client Muslims," known as *mawali* or non-Arab converts. Their status as foreigners excluded them from the kinship-based structure of Muslim society and all but excluded them from the protection of Muslim clans unless such clans voluntarily included them. In many respects, these client Muslims, although adherents to Islam, were treated as second-class citizens. Many of them were Persian (Iranian), and the center of Islamic culture shifted from Damascus to Baghdad, located on the Tigris River. The Umayyad managed to keep only Spain, flourishing there for the next three centuries but maintaining distinctive cultural differences from Muslims in the Middle East. The Abbasids blended Persian and Semitic culture to create a unique blend of Islamic culture.

The Abbasids introduced two innovations that changed the Islamic world. The first was assembling a military force consisting of slaves—Mamluks—that displaced the traditional Arabic and Persian army. Many of these Mamluks were Turkish horsemen, client Muslims who had not fared well under the Umayyad. The Mamluk force was created to ensure complete loyalty to the caliph and reduce the number of possible rivals to the throne. The embracing of a radical theology that advocated Muslim obedience to a single ruler brought about the second change. To advocate this theology, a university (The House of Wisdom) was founded. It was at this university that Islamic intellectualism began, an educational approach based on principles of rational inquiry. Literary and philosophical works from Greek and Indian writers were studied and debated there.

Despite the many advances made under its rule, the history of the later Abbasid dynasty is one of declining power. Although the Abbasid caliphs maintained nominal power until 1258, actual power passed to the Seljuk Turks some 200 years earlier. The Abbasids accelerated the breakup of a unified Islamic culture begun by the Umayyads. No longer would Islam be a distinct and clear cultural force based solely on the projection of an Arabic worldview. Instead, the political and cultural world of the Muslims became a collection of numerous independent groups, each with its own variant cultural and political heritage. The Muslim Empire began to decentralize and become more ethnic and local in nature, leading to the rise of competing Islamic centers.

THE MONGOLS

Another threat to Islam arrived with the Mongol invasions. Starting with Genghis and ending with Kublai, the Mongols had three great khans in the thirteenth century. The Khanate that ruled over Mesopotamia was called the Il-Khanate, one of four divisions of the Mongol Empire, and its power stretched down the eastern coastline of the Arabian Peninsula, north to the Armenian Mountains, westward to the edge of Palestine, and eastward to the Indian subcontinent. In modern terms, the Il-Khanate included parts of Saudi Arabia, Jordan, Syria, Turkmenistan, Afghanistan, Azerbaijan, and Pakistan, as well as all of Kuwait, Bahrain, Qatar, Iraq, and Iran. The Il-Khanate was immense and diverse, but it was just a portion of the Mongol Empire.

In Mesopotamia, the Mongols eventually converted to Islam, but this conversion did not take place until after the traditional powers in the region had been completely destroyed. The Mongol invaders won several victories over the Persians, beginning in 1221. As they moved westward, they killed most of those they conquered, often sparing only artisans or others who could contribute to their nomadic culture. By the 1250s, the Mongols were poised to challenge the Abbasid caliphate, which was centered in Baghdad. After defeating a small force of extreme Shiites known as the Assassins in northwestern Persia, the Mongol force turned its attention to the Abbasid capital and its caliph. Mongol troops were under orders to destroy the caliphate if it refused to surrender. When Baghdad refused to surrender, the Mongols laid siege to the city and sacked it in 1258.

Some scholars have surmised that the rift between Shiite and Sunni Muslims contributed to the Abbasid caliphate's inability to defend itself. The reigning caliph, Musta'sim, was Sunni and many of his subjects were Shiite and favored a change to Shiite government. Thus, it is possible to speculate that internal strife led to defections to the Mongol horde. Some historians go so far as to blame the caliph's Shiite vizier (his second in command) with aiding the enemy. Non-Muslims certainly joined in against the caliph as the Mongols advanced.

The caliph and the defenders within Baghdad soon found themselves surrounded and cut off from aid. Baghdad quickly fell, and Musta'sim was captured and executed. The Mongols killed all those who had not helped them in their victory. In fact, they consummated their victory with the unparalleled slaughter of some 800,000 people. The core of the Seljuk Turks was annihilated, and the Abbasid dynasty, which had ruled for 500 years, came to an immediate end. Henceforth, the Muslims in the region would follow one of three rising Islamic powers: the Mughal, the Ottoman, or the Safavid. No longer would the Persians, who had periodically and routinely ruled there, control the Tigris-Euphrates River valley.

Ironically, the Il-Khanate proved to be the shortest-lived of the Mongol khanates, lasting only about 80 years after the fall of Baghdad before their empire splintered into large ethnic fragments that each went its own way. Because the Mongols were nomadic, the obstacles to maintaining an empire as large as Mesopotamia after winning it were great—too great to over- come. Within a century, Mongol control of the region became untenable. The ruling khans converted to Islam around 1300. Following the 1335 death of the ruling khan, the khanate split into three separate states: the Turkish, Mongol, and Persian. Mesopotamia would eventually fall under the power of the Ottoman Turks who controlled the western portion of the old Il-Khanate.

THE OTTOMAN TURKS

The Ottoman Turks originated in Anatolia in what is now western Turkey, arriving there as settlers during the era of the Seljuk Turks (A.D. 1098–1308). In 1300, at about the time Seljuk power was waning, the Ottomans came to power. Although there were several Muslim states vying for power in the region, the Ottomans held their own and expanded their territory. By 1400, they controlled most of Anatolia and even held parts of the Byzantine Empire, including Bulgaria and Macedonia. The Ottomans committed themselves to bringing down Constantinople, a task that took until 1453 to complete. Once Constantinople—renamed Istanbul—fell, the Ottomans securely controlled the axis of east-west trade. Istanbul was made the capital of the Ottoman Empire, and it used its newly secured wealth to develop into a culturally refined and prosperous cosmopolitan center. The Ottomans continued to expand their empire, and by 1566, their gains included Mesopotamia. Ottoman efficiency and insistence upon justice were implemented in the Tigris-Euphrates River valley, much as they had been implemented in Egypt and other Ottoman territories. These territorial gains, however, were the last major successes the Ottomans would enjoy. The Ottoman Empire began to suffer a slow but steady decline that ended with the loss of most of its territories in the nineteenth and early twentieth centuries.

The decline of the Ottoman Empire can be attributed to three significant factors. After 1550, the Ottoman economy suffered, in part because of a shift in the Far East trade routes that bypassed the Middle East in favor of the Atlantic (and later Pacific) sea routes. Furthermore, changes in the administration of the Ottoman professional soldier class, the Janissaries, resulted in a weakened degree of loyalty to the central Ottoman power, limiting Istanbul's military capabilities. Finally, the Ottomans tenaciously clung to their military traditions and failed to adopt or counteract European innovations in military tactics and technology; this resulted in catastrophic losses on the battlefield. These factors weakened the empire, which began to be exploited by Austria and Russia by the late seventeenth century. Portions of the Ottomans' European holdings were periodically taken from them, and their weakening state led Czar Nicholas I of Russia to describe the Ottoman Empire as the "Sick Man of Europe." The ailing power proved unable to prevent European powers from taking not only its European territory but many of its territories in the Middle East as well, including Mesopotamia.

The invading forces of the Persians, Greeks, Muslims, Mongols, and Turks each left their mark on the Tigris-Euphrates River valleys. Persian architecture and Islamic belief helped give the region an identity, and each successive invading group adopted and sometimes improved the irrigation and canal systems of the rivers, further enhancing agricultural production and transportation within the region. Invading influences came and went, but the rivers remained steady and nearly unchanged. Each succeeding culture, however, left recognizable imprints in Mesopotamia that survived in the land between the rivers for centuries to come.

6

Mesopotamia in the Twentieth Century

WORLD WAR I

In 1914, war erupted in Europe. At the outset of World War I, few—if any—could have predicted that the Great War would impact Mesopotamia's future. Events proved otherwise. The Ottoman Turks allied themselves with Germany and the Austro-Hungarian Empire, forming what historians called the Central Powers. The end result of the war and negotiated peace was costly for each of the three powers, and the Ottoman state paid dearly for its role. Ottoman control over Middle Eastern territories was to be decided by the victors. In retrospect, the Middle East was undoubtedly up for grabs because of British and French involvement in the region during the war.

Great Britain's involvement in the region was associated with the activities of an archaeologist named Thomas Edward Lawrence, better known as Lawrence of Arabia. Lawrence was a graduate of Oxford and had spent time on an archaeological dig at Carchamish, located on the Euphrates River. When war broke out, Lawrence briefly worked for the Geographical Section of the General Staff in London. Later, he was dispatched to the Military Intelligence Department in Cairo. While in Cairo, he became an expert on Arab nationalist movements in the Ottoman provinces that are now Israel, Jordan, Lebanon, Syria, and the Hedjaz area of Saudi Arabia. He later served as the British liaison to the Arabs during the Arab revolt against the Ottoman Turks. Lawrence worked closely with an Arab leader named Faisal, who later held the thrones of Syria (briefly) and Iraq. Lawrence and his Arab allies successfully drove out Turkish forces from Palestine, Mesopotamia, and the Arabian Peninsula, ensuring Great Britain's role in the future of these territories.

THE ANGLO-FRENCH DECLARATION

At the close of World War I, control over Mesopotamia and the Fertile Crescent became hotly contested. In the Anglo-French

Thomas Edward Lawrence, also known as Lawrence of Arabia, helped drive out Turkish forces from Palestine, Mesopotamia, and the Arabian Peninsula during the Arab Revolt (1916–1918), and was a staunch supporter of Arab self-rule.

Declaration of November 7, 1918, France and Britain, two of the victorious European Allied powers, asserted their desire to establish legitimate "national governments and administrations deriving their authority from the initiative and free choice of the indigenous peoples"[29] in Syria and Iraq. It soon became apparent, however, that the two powers were more interested in exercising authority rather than transferring authority to the local populations. Back in Europe, T.E. Lawrence attended the Paris Peace Conference and argued unsuccessfully for Arab independence. Following the Treaty of Versailles and acting under authority of the League of Nations, France and Britain, in 1920, assumed control of Syria and Jordan, respectively. Britain was also given power to establish protectorates over other portions of the Middle East, including Palestine and what is now the state of Jordan. (Britain had unsuccessfully attempted to establish a protectorate over Iran in 1918.)

In June 1920, the British received their mandate over the Jordan region and proceeded to implement their centralized administrative reforms. Within weeks, rebellion broke out in the eastern portion of their mandate (modern-day Iraq) as tribesmen located near the Euphrates River rejected the notion of centralized British rule. The insurgents wanted to continue the Ottoman practice of decentralized administration of government. It took British forces several months to put down the rebellion. In the process, 450 British soldiers and almost 10,000 Iraqis lost their lives. Financially, the effort cost Britain some 40 million pounds. To safeguard against future rebellions, the British took drastic steps at the Cairo Conference of 1921. First, they divided the region into two different countries: Iraq and Jordan. (*Iraq* comes from the Arabic language and means "deep-rooted"). Next, they named the new rulers of the new countries. Both men were sons of Sharif Hussein, one of the key Arab leaders who had aided the British against the Turks during World War I. Faisal was named king of Iraq,

MESOPOTAMIAN ARCHAEOLOGY

In 1625, an Italian named Pietro della Valle visited the mound that contained the ancient city of Babylon and returned to Europe with some examples of ancient cuneiform. Scholars were interested in the pieces, but the inability to decipher the ancient script did little to encourage further exploration of the region. Then, in the 1750s, a few Mesopotamian artifacts were discovered and taken to Europe for analysis. These artifacts led to an increased interest in the ancient cultures of Mesopotamia, eventually culminating in numerous, competing archaeological excavations of ancient sites. (The subsequent widespread collection and removal of ancient artifacts was tantamount to looting, similar to what the ancient empires themselves had engaged in centuries before. Many Mesopotamian relics and works of art can be seen today in the British Museum in London and the Louvre in Paris.)

The 1840s bore witness to a rediscovery of the Mesopotamian cultures as waves of archaeological teams descended upon the region and excavated mounds that concealed the cities of old: Ur, Calah, Babylon, Nineveh, and others. Scholars from Britain and France initially led the way; later expeditions were organized by Germans and Americans. It was the Germans, relative latecomers to the region, who brought with them the organization and efficiency that redefined modern archaeology. Their most important innovation was the excavation and classification of different layers of archaeological sites; this allowed researchers to categorize and accurately date each civilization by strata. Prior to this improvement, excavators often conducted digs only in places that were likely to yield statues, precious metals, pottery, or other artifacts deemed valuable.

---

while his brother Abdullah became the amir of Jordan. Jordan, still part of the British mandate, was administrated from Palestine. Faisal had previously been the king of Syria, but the French had removed him within months of his installation. For his ascension to the Iraqi throne, Faisal was crowned in a decidedly British ceremony that featured the playing of Britain's national anthem, "God Save the King." Thus, Faisal became king of a Middle Eastern country that he had never

The early archaeologists faced intolerable heat, dust storms, lions, unscrupulous workers, and bands of menacing tribesmen who wanted to steal their horses. In spite of all these hazards, the nineteenth century was the era in which the ancient civilizations of Sumer, Babylonia, Assyria, and Persia came to life. The archaeological excavations generated excitement in Europe, leading to the birth of new fields of study and even changes in fashion. Scientific techniques were introduced and the study of cuneiform began in earnest.

After World War I, the Ottoman Turks lost Mesopotamia and other areas of the Middle East. The newly established League of Nations assigned Iraq to the protection of Great Britain, and the British placed all archaeological affairs under the direction of Gertrude Bell. The scholarly Bell was the daughter of a wealthy British industrialist and had been involved in Mesopotamian archaeological digs for several years before World War I. Bell oversaw the writing of a law that forbade shoddy expeditions. Henceforth, archaeological digs were allowed only if the expeditions were properly staffed with trained and experienced experts who would diligently preserve artifacts and ruins. The new breed of archaeologists was to include architects, epigraphists (those who specialize in copying and translating ancient inscriptions), and photographers. Bell also restricted dig sites to specific locations with narrowly defined limitations to prevent plundering. Under her leadership, the excavators and the new country of Iraq would share all archaeological finds, preserving them for the region from which they came. Concurrently, Bell established the Iraqi Antiquities Service to begin accumulating a collection of artifacts for a national Iraqi museum.

seen, installed by a European power to rule over a country he had never set foot in.

The manner in which the boundaries for these two countries were drawn is equally perplexing. Gertrude Bell, a low-level British diplomat who would later play a role in preserving ancient artifacts for the new state, drew the borders in 1918 on a whim, using a piece of tracing paper. Bell and T.E. Lawrence (Lawrence of Arabia), who was still hoping to see an independent

Arab state in the region, had worked together on plans to place Faisal on the throne of Iraq. Reflecting the roughly sketched map, three former provinces of the Ottoman Empire formed the heart of the newly fashioned Iraq: Basra, Baghdad, and Mosul. Basra, with a large Shiite population, was situated in the south and economically tied to Persian Gulf trade. Baghdad, which had strong Shiite ties (the province included the Shiite shrines of Karbala and Najaf), was located between Basra and Mosul and enjoyed ties to Persia (now Iran). Mosul, which had a large Kurdish population, was in the north and was historically more closely tied to Syria and Turkey than to the provinces of Baghdad or Basra. Time would reveal the complexity of maintaining this unlikely and forced unification of three distinct and competing provinces.

Events soon revealed the extreme difficulties facing the new nation. Three Kurdish revolts occurred between 1922 and 1932; another uprising erupted in the south in 1935–36. Political factions vied for power, with little prospect of instilling stability. There were more than 50 different governments that gained and lost power in 37 years (1921–1958). Many of these factions arose through military coups. Thus, the practice of strong military figures seizing power was well established before the emergence of Saddam Hussein in 1979. Great Britain continued its role in the protectorate until Iraq was declared independent in 1932.

The following year witnessed great accomplishments as well as instability. Iraq became the first Arab nation to be admitted into the League of Nations; King Faisal died; one of Iraq's ethnic groups, the Assyrians, revolted but were overwhelmingly defeated; and Britain and Iraq signed an oil agreement. While the young country began to fend for itself, instability and the power-by-force trend of the 1920s again resurfaced. Iraq suffered its first of many modern military coups on October 29, 1936. Over the next several months, the coup was followed by assassinations of a few high-ranking officials in the new government, including the new dictator, who was killed in August 1937.

THE BA'ATH PARTY

In 1941, a former Iraqi prime minister, Rashid Ali, successfully overthrew the government with the support of the military. Ali then looked to Adolph Hitler's Germany for aid. German influence, new to the region, was enabled by circumstances in Europe. World War II had erupted and France had surrendered to Germany. The Vichy government, little more than a puppet regime of the Nazis, now ruled parts of France and French territories. It usually supported Nazi activities, as was the case in the Middle East. Thus, the French mandate territories of Lebanon and Syria began to show signs of Nazi influence. The Ba'ath (Arabic for "Renaissance," "Rebirth," or "Resurrection") Party in Syria became enamored of some of the Nazi concepts, especially to Nazi anti-Semitism. Because the Ba'ath Party sought to reestablish Arab supremacy and opposed the creation of a Jewish state in Palestine, it was open to Nazi presence in the Middle East. Great Britain, led by Prime Minister Winston Churchill, recognized the growing threat and seized the initiative. (For additional information on this political party, enter "Ba'ath Party" into any search engine and browse the many sites listed.)

British forces occupied Lebanon and Syria, simultaneously squelching Rashid Ali's rebellion just one month after the coup. British troops remained in Iraq until after World War II. Following the end of the war, Great Britain reestablished the monarchy, placing Prince Abdallah on the throne as regent for his nephew Faisal II, the grandson of Faisal I and the cousin of Jordan's King Hussein. Faisal II, who had inherited Iraq's throne at the age of four when his father died in 1939, was to assume the throne in his own right when he came of age in 1953.

Iraq joined the newly formed Arab League in March 1945. The group's stated purpose was to defend Palestine; specifically, the Arab League vowed to fight against any attempts to establish an independent Jewish state in Palestine. At the same time, the Ba'ath Party was committed to forming a unified Arab state founded upon socialism. Members of the party also favored nonalignment during the Cold War era and were opposed to any form of European colonialism in the Middle East.

In 1955, the Ba'ath position was sidestepped when the Cold War came to the Middle East with the signing of the Baghdad Pact, an anti-Soviet defensive alliance signed by Iraq, Turkey, Iran, Pakistan, and the United Kingdom (Britain). Although the United States did not join the group, it did pledge to work with it in the event of war with the Soviet Union.

The events of July 14, 1958, forever altered the future course of Iraq's history when a military coup d'etat, led by General Abd al-Karim Qasim, who had close ties to the Iraqi Communist Party, succeeded in overthrowing the monarchy. King Faisal II, who had ascended to the throne in 1953, was summarily executed, together with the crown prince and Chief Minister Nuri al-Said.

Then, in 1961, Great Britain granted independence to Kuwait, a small country bordering Iraq. The new government of Iraq refused to recognize Kuwait as an independent country, claiming the territory belonged to Iraq. After Iraq massed armed forces on the Iraqi-Kuwaiti border, Britain sent troops to defend the small Arab kingdom. Iraqi authorities reconsidered and proceeded to back down, diffusing the crisis.

In March 1963, Ba'athists in Iraq briefly seized control of the government there and executed Qasim. The dream of uniting Syria, Egypt, and Iraq—a major policy proposal of the Ba'ath Party platform in each of the three countries—seemed plausible. The Ba'athists in Iraq, however, were soon forced to relinquish power when they could not stand up to a new force led by

A group of Ba'athist guerrillas advances past a parade stand in Baghdad in celebration of the first anniversary of the Ba'athist Party taking power in Iraq in 1968. The party ruled in Iraq until Saddam Hussein was deposed in 2003.

Abd al-Salam Arif. All talk of unification ended with purges—in both Syria and Iraq—of Ba'ath Party members. Five years later, the situation was reversed when the Ba'ath Party successfully seized power in Iraq with the help of the military. This marked the merging of the Ba'ath Party and the state government, a process whereby most important government functions became synonymous with the party, including the armed forces, intelligence, and police.

IRAQ AND IRAN

Saddam Hussein became Iraq's president in 1979 after having been a faithful member of the Ba'ath Party for at least 20 years.

In 1959, he fled to Egypt after taking part in an assassination attempt on Iraq's prime minister. While in Egypt, he attended law school. When the Ba'athists seized power in 1963, Hussein returned to Iraq. Later, he played a vital role in the 1968 seizure of power by the Ba'ath Party. He had also held key political and economic posts in the government before becoming president of Iraq. As president, Hussein sought to improve Iraq's standing in the Arab world. To this end, he strengthened the country's oil industry and expanded its military. Other Muslim nations and the West viewed Iraq's new military might with apprehension, and tension mounted.

To make matters worse, Iraq had managed to entangle itself in the problems of its neighbor, Iran. The Nuzhih Plot, which was a plan to overthrow the new Iranian republic, was uncovered and thwarted on July 9, 1980. A purge of the Iranian military led by Ayatollah Ruhollah Khomeini cracked down on insurgents and potential opposition. Evidence surfaced that implicated the Iraqi government, elevating tensions between the two countries. In reality, the conflict was merely an extension of past animosities and hatred between the two countries.

Iraq invaded Iran in September 1980. Saddam Hussein's regime cited several grievances with Iran as justification for the invasion. The two countries share a border, which measures some 750 miles and is routinely disputed. The most contentious of these border disputes involved claims over the Shatt al-Arab —the conjoined Tigris and Euphrates Rivers—which empties into the northern end of the Persian Gulf. An attempt to avoid one of these border conflicts had culminated in a 1975 treaty, the Algiers Agreement, in which Iran and Iraq agreed to share the river, partitioning it in the middle. The new conflict between Iraq and Iran focused on other border issues. Iraq wished to regain three disputed islands in the Strait of Hormuz (located in the Persian Gulf), which Iran had taken possession of in 1971. Furthermore, Iraq claimed some of the mountainous territory in western Iran along the border separating the two countries. Iraq's government was also frightened that the new Iranian Shiite regime might inflame its own Shiite population in southern Iraq to revolt.

The resulting conflict, the Iran-Iraq War, lasted until 1988. The effects of the war were devastating, but there were other changes in Iraq during the 1980s. Politically, the ideals of a socialist state—one of the underpinnings of Ba'athism—were largely ignored as the country's economy shifted toward capitalism, spurred on by oil sales and the need to supply the military machine during the war with Iran. During this decade, the party also shifted much of its emphasis from Arab nationalism to an unambiguous emphasis on Iraqi nationalism. Despite this subtle shift, the party often claimed to represent the true Arab nation; though Iraq continued to have hostile relations with neighboring Arab countries.

THE GULF WAR AND THE FALL OF SADDAM HUSSEIN

In August 1990, a mere two years after the war with Iran ended, Saddam Hussein invaded Iraq's neighbor to the south, Kuwait. This invasion stirred up the international community, which ultimately forced the withdrawal of Iraqi forces from the small country in February 1991 during the Gulf War. Following this conflict, Hussein suppressed a rebellion of the Kurds in northern Iraq and a Shiite uprising in southern Iraq. While putting down the Kurdish revolt, Hussein's forces used chemical agents to wipe out the northern Kurdish village of Halabja.

Throughout the 1990s, Iraq faced economic sanctions imposed by the international community for the country's failure to comply with weapons inspections as agreed to at the end of the Gulf War. Continued noncompliance with United Nations resolutions resulted in the U.S.-led invasion of Iraq that began on March 20, 2003, and forced Saddam Hussein from power. Three cities located on the Tigris and Euphrates

Rivers proved to be strategically important: Umm Qasr, Nassiriya, and Baghdad. Coalition forces seized Umm Qasr, a key port city located on the Shatt al-Arab—the combined Tigris and Euphrates Rivers as they flow into the Persian Gulf. During the invasion, U.S. forces also defeated an Iraqi force at Nassiriya, a key city strategically situated on the Euphrates River about 225 miles south of Baghdad. After routing Iraqi defenses, U.S. troops managed to cross the Euphrates unhindered, paving the way for the capture of Baghdad. Coalition forces arrived at the outskirts of Baghdad on April 2 and seized control of its airport the next day. With the fall of the Iraqi capital, much of the organized military resistance dissipated, although smaller attacks against coalition forces have continued through 2004. Saddam Hussein fled shortly after the hostilities began; his whereabouts were unknown until December 2003 when he was captured. Currently, he is being held by the new Iraqi government and facing charges for crimes against humanity.

7

The Modern Rivers' Impact on Iraq, Syria, and Turkey

Since ancient times, irrigation has been essential for agricultural food production in Mesopotamia. Despite the conveniences of modern technology, people living on the Tigris-Euphrates plain still rely on irrigation, even in its ancient and primitive forms, in order to raise crops.

Although dams are utilized to siphon off water through canals to irrigate fields, and the impounded waters are valuable as a means of producing electricity, some irrigation practices date back to the time of Sumer. Northern Mesopotamia can depend upon some rain, at least early in the growing season, but agriculture in southern Mesopotamia relies solely on the waters from the Tigris and Euphrates. Irrigation techniques include the digging of transverse trenches, the shadoof, and types of windlass. These technologies date back to ancient times. The Greek historian Herodotus identified one of these when he described irrigation in Mesopotamia:

> Very little rain falls in the land of Assyria, and this little is what nourishes the root of the crop; but it is in its watering from the river that the corn (*sitos*) crop wins its ripeness and the bread grain comes into being. It is not as in Egypt, where the river itself rises over the fields; in Babylon the watering is done by hand-operated swing beams. For all the Babylonian country, as in the case of Egypt, is cut up with canals. . . .[30]

The "swing beams" described by Herodotus are probably the shadoof, "a long wooden pole secured at a fulcrum to a horizontal beam of wood, supported at each end by a timber pole or a mud-brick column. The short end of the lever was counterweighted with a stone or a lump of clay, with the bucket attached by a rope to the other end."[31] The windlass is simply a water-lifting machine consisting of a cylinder or drum wound with rope and turned by a crank. In agriculture, the windlass raises water for irrigation purposes. Scholars believe that this technology is almost as old as the civilization that first developed in Mesopotamia.

WATER AND POLITICS

The use of water and issues regarding water rights among the countries of the region stir much controversy over the rivers today. The Tigris and Euphrates flow through three countries: Turkey, Syria, and Iraq. The bulk of each of the rivers is found in Iraq, but one of the most serious issues facing Iraq is the use of water upstream in Syria and Turkey. Since water resources are scarce in the Middle East, there is a legitimate concern that Turkey and Syria will use up most of the water before it ever flows into Iraq.

Because both rivers begin in Turkey, that country lays claim to both the Tigris and the Euphrates. Syria and Iraq, however, are both dependent upon these rivers for their irrigation needs, and Iraq maintains that water from the Tigris and Euphrates, which has been used to irrigate Mesopotamia for thousands of years, should not be obstructed from the Iraqi plain.

Most of the disputes among Turkey, Syria, and Iraq center on dams and who is able to control the rivers' flow. Iraq has seven dams in use, but concern for water control was not a priority under Saddam Hussein, and Iraqi irrigation already reduces the flow of the Tigris before it reaches the Shatt al-Arab. With U.S. attempts to establish a new government in Iraq, water issues are sure to be of paramount importance.

Since 1990, Turkey has been engaged in the largest development project in its history. The Southeast Anatolia Development Project includes plans to construct 22 dams and 19 power plants by 2005. Through this program, Turkey intends to irrigate about 30,000 square miles of parched land. Turkey aspires to produce enough crops to feed much of the Middle East. Although the project is behind schedule, there have been several dams constructed, including the Ataturk Dam, which

(continued on page 98)

MARSH ARABS

The Marsh Arabs, or the Madan people (sometimes spelled Ma'dan or Ma'adan), live in the marshlands of what is present-day southern Iraq. The marshlands cover about 3,860 square miles and are the largest wetlands in the Middle East. They are also one of the most exceptional freshwater ecosystems in the world. Small branches from the Tigris and Euphrates Rivers that break off into the level plain help form the marshlands. For centuries, annual flooding created seasonal marshes and helped water the permanent wetlands.

The Madans are descendants of the Sumerians and live virtually the same way their ancestors lived some 5,000 years ago. Today, the Madans dwell in a remote, harsh environment that experiences relatively cold and rainy winters, strong thunderstorms and potential flooding each spring, and hot summers with temperatures that can reach 125 degrees Fahrenheit. Throughout the year, especially in the summer, the region is subjected to high winds. Despite the climate and the inhospitable environment in which they live, the Madans have consistently adapted and thrived in the marshlands.

The Marsh Arabs are sometimes called the "people of the reeds" because of their reliance upon the tall, thick reeds found in the wetlands. The rushes are used as poles to maneuver their canoes (*mashuf*) through the channels and lagoons of the marshes. The reeds are also utilized to weave baskets, make beds, erect fences, and fashion mats. Their houses, known as *mudhif*, sit on small islands and are also made from the abundant reeds. These long, narrow structures have arched roofs and seldom have windows. Similar reed houses are mentioned in Sumerian records dating back to 4000 B.C.

Marsh Arabs gather food and supplies from the wetlands in which they live. They catch fish, hunt waterfowl, gather reeds and grasses for weaving mats and baskets, and grow rice and dates in the marshes. Marsh Arabs also rely on the water buffalo, an animal indigenous to the wetlands, for many of their needs. The Madans keep the animals near their homes, making use of the animals' milk from which they also make butter. The water buffalo also produce dung, which supplies fuel and a substance that is naturally waterproof. The water buffalo dung is formed into plate-shaped patties that are dried and stacked in piles for storage. These dried patties are then burned in Madan ovens. Wet dung is also used to seal woven baskets that are used for grain storage and to patch small holes in the roofs and walls of Madan homes.

The future of this unique and peculiar way of life is very much in doubt. There were about 500,000 Marsh Arabs in southern Iraq before Iraq invaded Kuwait in 1990. After the end of the 1991 Gulf War, Saddam Hussein's regime began diverting water away from the marshes. Banks lining the channels that siphon off the Tigris prevent flooding that once inundated the marshes, and a newly constructed canal diverts the waters of virtually the entire Euphrates, completely circumventing the marshes. These diversions have prevented about two-thirds of the water that once reached the wetlands from entering the marshes. As a result, two of the three primary marsh areas (al-Qurnah and al-Hammar) have experienced an 85 percent environmental degradation. The third (Hawr al-Hawizeh), which borders Iran, is partially watered by Iranian rivers but has still suffered an estimated 65 percent degradation. Facing starvation, an estimated 200,000 Marsh Arabs have fled the region, many to refugee camps in Iran. The drainage efforts have been called "a crime against humanity" and "the deliberate extinction of one of the oldest races in the world."*

Saddam Hussein initiated the diversion efforts to squelch resistance to his government, claiming the Shiite rebels found aid and were hiding in the marshes. The dictator also claimed that the drainage projects were necessary to guarantee adequate water resources for the agricultural needs of central Iraq. Since the U.S.-led invasion of Iraq in March 2003, there have been some attempts made to restore the wetlands. The task is daunting, and many experts believe much of the damage is probably irreversible. It is likely that if the draining continues or cannot be reversed, the unique and ancient culture of the Marsh Arabs will be lost forever.

* Afshin Molavi, "Iraq's Eden: Reviving the Legendary Marshes," *National Geographic News*, May 1, 2003. Available online at *http://news.nationalgeographic.com/news/2003/05/0501_030501_arabmarshes.html*.

Syria's Euphrates Dam, which is used to harness the waters of its namesake, opened in 1973 and generates 30 percent of the country's electricity. However, the dam has limited the amount of water that flows into Iraq, and the two countries were on the verge of war in the mid-1970s due to Syria's monopolization of the Euphrates' water.

(continued from page 95)

ranks as the world's sixth-largest dam and is designed to withstand earthquakes of 8.0 on the Richter scale. In the face of opposition from environmental groups, both domestic and foreign, the government of Turkey has continued the program in the hopes of enhancing the economy of southeastern Turkey, which has struggled in the modern global economy. This region is home to Turkey's Kurdish minority.

Syria has fewer options for harnessing water because a smaller amount of water from the Tigris and Euphrates Rivers flows through the country than through either Turkey or Iraq. Because Turkey controls the rivers upstream, Syria is often at the mercy of its northern neighbor. For example, when the Ataturk Dam opened in January 1990, Turkey blocked the Euphrates for a month. Syria was left with a quarter of the flow needed to run one of its hydroelectric plants. During that month, Syria's Al-Thawra plant managed to produce a paltry 12 percent of the electricity needed.

Syria has also engaged in dam construction. In the 1960s, several dams were built on the Euphrates River in the 1960s. The Euphrates Dam, also known as the Tabaqah Dam, opened in 1973 and supplies 30 percent of Syria's electricity. Water from the dam's reservoir (Lake Assad) is used for the irrigation of cotton, barley, tobacco, vegetables, and wheat. In addition, Syrian authorities have also dammed two tributaries leading into the Euphrates. Iraq protested the building of the Euphrates Dam, insisting that it so reduced the flow of the Euphrates that more than 3 million Iraqi farmers could no longer irrigate their fields. (No Syrian dams have been built on the Tigris, which flows through the country for only 30 miles.)

Despite regime changes and technological innovations throughout the history of the eastern Fertile Crescent, there has been one constant in the region: the life-giving flow of the waters of the Tigris and Euphrates Rivers. Today, the Tigris and the Euphrates continue to live out their destiny.

c. 4500 b.c.	Cuneiform writing invented.
c. 3500	Sumerian city-states develop in southern Mesopotamia.
1792–1750	Hammurabi rules Babylon, controlling most of Mesopotamia.
1600	The Hittites invade and plunder Babylonia.
1595	The Kassites occupy and control Babylonia for nearly 400 years.
1350	Assyrians rise to prominence in Mesopotamia.
1157	Elamite invaders overthrow last of the Kassite rulers.
1124	Nebuchadnezzar I forces Elamites out of Babylonia.

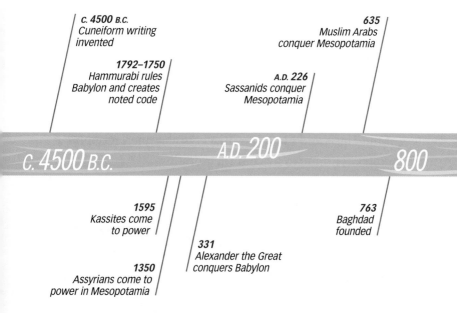

c. 4500 B.C.
Cuneiform writing
invented

1792–1750
Hammurabi rules
Babylon and creates
noted code

635
Muslim Arabs
conquer Mesopotamia

A.D. 226
Sassanids conquer
Mesopotamia

c. 4500 B.C.   *A.D. 200*   *800*

1595
Kassites come
to power

1350
Assyrians come to
power in Mesopotamia

331
Alexander the Great
conquers Babylon

763
Baghdad
founded

1100	Babylonian forces successfully invade Assyria but fail to capture the capital city of Ashur.
745	Assyrians, led by Tiglath-Pileser III, assert control over the region.
612	Nineveh sacked by Medes and Babylonians; Assyrian Empire falls.
605–561	Nebuchadnezzar II reigns; Babylonia enjoys renovation of temples, palaces, and other public buildings, and territorial expansion.
539	Babylon falls to Cyrus the Great, who adds it to the Persian Empire.
c. 350	After the course of the Euphrates River shifts, the city of Ur disappears, eventually being covered by the shifting sand.

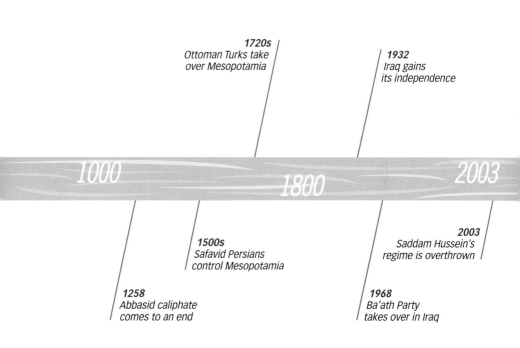

1720s
Ottoman Turks take over Mesopotamia

1932
Iraq gains its independence

1000

1800

2003

1500s
Safavid Persians control Mesopotamia

2003
Saddam Hussein's regime is overthrown

1258
Abbasid caliphate comes to an end

1968
Ba'ath Party takes over in Iraq

331   Alexander the Great conquers Babylon.

312   Seleucus succeeds Alexander; Babylon begins to slowly decline.

247   Parthians overthrow Seleucids.

A.D. 224   Sassanids overthrow Parthians.

640   Muslim Arabs bring Sassanid rule to an end.

763   Baghdad is founded, eventually leading to the repositioning of the center of the Muslim world from Damascus to Mesopotamia.

1055   Mesopotamia, along with Persia, is added to the Great Seljuk state; Seljuk sultans become de facto leaders of the Abbasid caliphate in Baghdad.

1258   Baghdad falls to Mongols, marking the end of the Abbasid caliphate.

1500s   Safavid Persians control Mesopotamia and rule from Baghdad.

1720s   Ottoman Turks wrest control of Mesopotamia from the Safavid Persians.

1840   The first of many Mesopotamian archaeological excavations begins.

1932   Iraq, which includes most of Mesopotamia, gains its independence; Iraq becomes the first Arab nation to be admitted into the League of Nations.

1945   Syria, which includes northern portions of Mesopotamia, gains its independence.

1967   Iraq fights against Israel in the Six-Day War.

1968   Ba'ath Party seizes power in Iraq.

1979	Saddam Hussein becomes president of Iraq.
1980–1988	War waged between Iraq and Iran.
1990	Iraq invades Kuwait.
1991	Multinational force drives Iraqi forces out of Kuwait.
1990s	Saddam Hussein's regime drains Iraq's marshlands in an effort to defeat resistance.
2003	Saddam Hussein's regime is overthrown.
2004	Provisional Iraqi government takes control on June 28.

CHAPTER 1:
The Twin Rivers of the Eastern Fertile Crescent

1 John P. McKay, Bennett D. Hill, John Buckler, and Patricia Buckley Ebrey, *A History of World Societies*, 6th ed. (Boston, Mass.: Houghton Mifflin, 2004), 12.

2 Morris Jastrow, Jr., *The Civilization of Babylonia and Assyria: Its Remains, Language, History, Religion, Commerce, Law, Art, and Literature* (Philadelphia, Pa.: J.B. Lippincott, 1915), 7.

3 *http://www.ancientroute.com/water/tigrisrv.htm.*

4 Statistics found at *http://www.jameswbell.com/a013marshreclamation.html* and Morris Jastrow, Jr., *The Civilization of Babylonia and Assyria*, 7.

CHAPTER 2:
The Emergence of the First Civilization

5 Linda Civitello, *Cuisine and Culture: A History of Food and People* (Hoboken, N.J.: John Wiley & Sons, 2004), 9.

6 Ibid.

7 *Sumer: Cities of Eden* (Alexandria, Va.: Time-Life Books, 1993), 35.

8 Mark W. Chavalas, ed., *The Ancient World: Prehistory–476 C.E.*, Vol. 1: *c. 25,000 B.C.E.–312 B.C.E.* (Pasadena, Calif.: Salem Press, 2004), 128.

CHAPTER 3:
Southern Mesopotamia: The Early Babylonian Empire

9 Clarice Swisher, *The Ancient Near East* (San Diego, Calif.: Lucent Books, 1995), 64.

10 Claude Hermann Walter Johns, M.A. Litt. D. Master of St. Catharine's College, Cambridge, U.K. Lecturer in Assyriology, Queens' College, Cambridge, and King's College, London. Author of *Assyrian Deeds and Documents of the 7th Century B.C.; The Oldest Code of Laws; Babylonian and Assyrian Laws; Contracts and Letters*; etc. Found at *http://www.yale.edu/lawweb/avalon/medieval/hammpre.htm.*

11 Ibid.

12 Ibid.

13 *http://www.fordham.edu/halsall/ancient/hamcode.html.*

14 Ibid.

15 Ibid.

16 H.W.F. Saggs, *The Greatness That Was Babylon: A Sketch of the Ancient Civilization of the Tigris-Euphrates Valley* (New York: Hawthorn Books, 1962), 413–414.

17 Ibid., 414.

CHAPTER 4:
The Assyrian Empire

18 James Wellard, *Babylon* (New York: Saturday Review Press, 1972), 140.

19 Samuel Noah Kramer and the editors of Time-Life Books, *Cradle of Civilization* (Alexandria, Va.: Time-Life Books, 1978), 57.

20 Ibid.

21 Wellard, 142.

22 Kramer and the Editors of Time-Life, 58.

23 Ibid.

24 Ibid., 61.

25 Ibid., 61–62.

CHAPTER 5:
Persians, Greeks, Muslims, Mongols, and Turks

26 Norman F. Cantor, *Antiquity: The Civilization of the Ancient World* (New York: HarperCollins, 2003), 5.

27 Georges Roux, *Ancient Iraq* (Cleveland, Ohio: The World Publishing Company, 1964), 355.

28 Jastrow, 185.

CHAPTER 6:
Mesopotamia in the Twentieth Century

29 Fred J. Khouri, *The Arab-Israeli Dilemma* (Syracuse, N.Y.: Syracuse University Press, 1968), 361.

CHAPTER 7:
The Modern Rivers' Impact on Iraq, Syria, and Turkey

30 P.R.S. Moorey, *Ancient Mesopotamian Materials and Industries: The Archaeological Evidence* (Oxford, U.K.: Clarendon Press, 1994), 1.

31 Ibid., 4.

Adler, Philip J. *World Civilizations.* 3rd ed. Belmont, Calif.: Thomson Wadsworth, 2003.

Bertman, Stephen. *Handbook to Life in Ancient Mesopotamia.* New York: Facts on File, 2003.

Brackman, Arnold C. *The Luck of Nineveh: Archaeology's Great Adventure.* New York: McGraw-Hill, 1978.

Cantor, Norman F. *Antiquity: The Civilization of the Ancient World.* New York: HarperCollins 2003.

Cavendish, Marshall. *Encyclopedia of World Geography: The Middle East.* 2nd ed., Vol. 15. New York: Andromeda Oxford Limited, 2002.

Chavalas, Mark W., ed. *The Ancient World: Prehistory—476 C.E.* Vol. 1: *c. 25,000 B.C.E.–312 B.C.E.* Pasadena, Calif.: Salem Press, 2004.

Chiera, Edward. *They Wrote on Clay: The Babylonian Tablets Speak Today.* Chicago, Ill.: The University of Chicago Press, Phoenix Books, 1938.

Civitello, Linda. *Cuisine and Culture: A History of Food and People.* Hoboken, N.J.: John Wiley & Sons, 2004.

Conklin, Edward. *Getting Back into the Garden of Eden.* Lanham, Md.: University Press of America, 1998.

Hammerton, Sir J.A., ed. *Wonders of the Past.* Vol. 1. New York: Wise and Company, 1948.

Harris, George L. *Iraq: Its People, Its Society, Its Culture.* New Haven, Conn.: Hraf Press, 1958.

Hawkes, Jacquetta. *The First Great Civilizations: Life in Mesopotamia, the Indus Valley, and Egypt.* New York: Alfred A. Knopf, 1973.

Heravi, Mehdi, ed. *Concise Encyclopedia of the Middle East.* Washington, D.C.: Public Affairs Press, 1973.

Hicks, Jim. *The Persians.* Amsterdam: Time-Life Books, 1976.

Jastrow, Morris, Jr. *The Civilization of Babylonia and Assyria: Its Remains, Language, History, Religion, Commerce, Law, Art, and Literature.* Philadelphia, Pa.: J.B. Lippincott Company, 1915.

Khouri, Fred J. *The Arab-Israeli Dilemma*. Syracuse, N.Y.: Syracuse University Press, 1968.

Kramer, Samuel Noah. *Cradle of Civilization*. Alexandria, Va.: Time-Life Books, 1978.

———. *The Sumerians: Their History, Culture, and Character*. Chicago, Ill.: The University of Chicago Press, 1963.

Maisels, Charles Keith. *The Near East: Archaeology in the "Cradle of Civilization."* London: Routledge, 1993.

McKay, John P., Bennett D. Hill, John Buckler, and Patricia Buckley Ebrey. *A History of World Societies*. 6th ed. Boston, Mass.: Houghton Mifflin, 2004.

Moorey, P.R.S. *Ancient Mesopotamian Materials and Industries: The Archaeological Evidence*. Oxford, U.K.: Clarendon Press, 1994.

———. *Ur' of the Chaldees': A Revised and Updated Edition of Sir Leonard Woolley's Excavations at Ur*. Ithaca, N.Y.: Cornell University Press, 1982.

Oppenheim, A. Leo. *Ancient Mesopotamia: Portrait of a Dead Civilization*. Chicago, Ill.: The University of Chicago Press, 1964.

Roux, Georges. *Ancient Iraq*. Cleveland, Ohio.: The World Publishing Company, 1964.

Saggs, H.W.F. *The Greatness That Was Babylon: A Sketch of the Ancient Civilization of the Tigris-Euphrates Valley*. New York: Hawthorn Books, 1962.

Sumer: Cities of Eden. Alexandria, Va.: Time-Life Books, 1993.

Swisher, Clarice. *The Ancient Near East*. San Diego, Calif.: Lucent Books, 1995.

Wellard, James. *Babylon*. New York: Saturday Review Press, 1972.

FURTHER READING

Chesney, Francis R. *Expedition for the Survey of the Rivers Euphrates-Tigris,* Carried out by Order of the British Government in the Years 1835–1837. Westport, Conn.: Greenwood Publishing Group, Inc., 1970.

Finegan, Jack. *Archaeological History of the Ancient Middle East.* Boulder, Colo.: Westview Press, 1979.

Moorey, P.R.S. *Ancient Mesopotamian Materials and Industries: The Archaeological Evidence.* Oxford, U.K.: Oxford University Press, 1994.

Saggs, H.F.W. *Babylonians.* Berkeley, Calif.: University of California Press, 2000.

WEBSITES

Tigris River Geography
http://www.ancientroute.com/water/tigrisrv.htm

Code of Hammurabi
http://www.fordham.edu/halsall/ancient/hamcode.html

The Tigris-Euphrates Marshlands
http://www.jameswbell.com/a013marshreclamation.html

Lawrence of Arabia
http://www.lawrenceofarabia.info

SHANE MOUNTJOY is an Associate Professor of History at York College in York, Nebraska, where he resides with his wife Vivian and their four daughters. Professor Mountjoy teaches college-level history, geography, and political science courses. He earned an Associate of Arts degree from York College, a Bachelor of Arts degree from Lubbock Christian University, a Master of Arts from the University of Nebraska-Lincoln, and a Doctor of Philosophy from the University of Missouri-Columbia. He has been teaching for fifteen years.

TIM McNEESE is an Associate Professor of History at York College in York, Nebraska, where he is currently in his thirteenth year of instruction. Professor McNeese earned an Associate of Arts degree from York College, a Bachelor of Arts in history and political science from Harding University, and a Master of Arts in history from Southwest Missouri State University.

A prolific author of books for elementary, middle and high school, and college readers, McNeese has published more than 70 books and educational materials over the past 20 years, on everything from Indian mythology to the building of the Great Wall of China. His writing has earned him a citation in the library reference work, *Something about the Author*. His wife, Beverly, is an Assistant Professor of English at York College and the couple has two children, Noah and Summer. Readers are encouraged to contact Professor McNeese at tdmcneese@york.edu.